THE
TECH
THAT
COMES
NEXT

Amy Sample Ward
Afua Bruce

THE
TECH
THAT
COMES
NEXT

How Changemakers, Philanthropists, and Technologists

Can Build an Equitable World

WILEY

Published by John Wiley & Sons, Inc., Hoboken, New Jersey.
Published simultaneously in Canada.

For general information on our other products and services or for technical support, please contact our
Customer Care Department within the United States at (800) 762-2974, outside the United States at
(317) 572-3993 or fax (317) 572-4002.

Wiley also publishes its books in a variety of electronic formats. Some content that appears in print may
not be available in electronic formats. For more information about Wiley products, visit our web site at
www.wiley.com.

Library of Congress Cataloging-in-Publication Data is Available:

ISBN: 9781119859819 (Cloth)
ISBN: 9781119859826 (ePub)
ISBN: 9781119859833 (ePDF)

Cover Design: Wiley
Cover Image: © The7Dew/Getty Images

SKY10032489_012622

To the NTEN team: Andrea, Ash, Dan, Drew, Eileigh, Jarlisa, Jeremy, Jude, Karl, Leana, Michelle, Pattie, Samara, Thomas, and Tristan: You inspire me every day and remind me that together we can change ourselves and our world.

—Amy

To the many friends and colleagues and mentors who have encouraged me over the years to pursue making a difference at the intersection of technology and community;

To my parents, who taught me at a young age what it means to be a part of a community, and to my sisters, who have always kept me humble;
Thank you.

—Afua

Contents

Acknowledgments

This book was written and edited on the unceded traditional territories of the Cowlitz, the Clackamas, the Confederated Tribes of the Grand Ronde, and the Confederated Tribes of Siletz Indians; the Nacotchtank (Anacostan) and the Piscataway; and the Ohlone, Muwekma, and Ramaytush peoples—the original and rightful stewards of the lands also known as Portland, Oregon; Washington, DC; and San Francisco, California. To the Indigenous communities who were here before us, those with whom we live today, and the seven generations to come, we are grateful for your leadership and stewardship. To our non-Indigenous readers, the work we do and that we discuss in this book requires that we be committed to the process of truth and reconciliation so that we can make a better future for all. We ask you to join us in that commitment, and we encourage you to learn more about the native land where you live, work, and explore, and to support the Indigenous communities in your area. (Learn more at www.native-land.ca.)

We recognize the access to insights, research, and experiences we have and that we have brought to this book because of our current work at NTEN, where Amy is the CEO, and DataKind, where Afua is the Chief Program Officer. While our work has enabled us to learn and grow, it has also informed many of our ideas and our hope for what is possible for the future.

Deep gratitude both to Kirsten Janene-Nelson for doing more than editing our work and truly partnering with us to convey our ideas as well as possible, and to Michelle Samplin-Salgado for helping us find ways to use visualizations to bring ideas to life beyond words. Thank you to both of you for contributing your talents and heart in this project.

Thank you to all of the individuals we interviewed for sharing your ideas and experience with us. Thank you to the artists who made their illustrations and fonts available for use, including Natalia Nesterenko for the characters and Tré Seals of Vocal Type Co. for the Bayard typeface. Your work inspires us. Your work matters. You matter.

Thanks to the many individuals, especially women of color, who have worked so hard to study the ways people have been harmed or overlooked by mainstream technology development—and then to reveal their findings and advocate for change. This necessary work inspires us, protects everyone, and pushes technology to be relevant and responsible to all.

This book would not have been possible without the dedication, service, and contributions to the field of all those quoted and highlighted here—as well as the contributions of the multitudes of others whose work actively makes our world better.

We want to acknowledge the privilege we have in being able to put this book together. We also acknowledge that our thoughts, ideas, and recommendations are inherently informed by the long journey toward equity that has been led by Black, Indigenous, and other communities of color, by disabled people, LGBTQIA2+ people, immigrants and refugees and their children, poor people, tired people, and so many others. We can do our work today only because of the struggles and victories for rights that so many have dedicated their lives to—and we do this work now in service to the changes we know are possible when we work together.

Introduction

Welcome. Thank you. And hello.

We wrote this book for everyone; or, rather, for anyone. For anyone who thought there could be another way, there could be better outcomes, there could be different models to try. We hope that is you, so, welcome. And thank you for being here.

In the many conversations we have had with practitioners across many sectors during the development of this book, we found ourselves repeating a number of the same points about how to talk about the organizations, people, and systems involved in the work of using and building technology for changing the world. In the same spirit of those open and honest conversations, we want to invite you into some of the thinking and framing that shaped this book.

WHY US?

Both of us have worked in a diversity of spaces, including advocacy organizations, government, industry, and nonprofits—in the fields of philanthropy, capacity-building, and policymaking. Through our work as strategists, organizers, researchers, technologists, and policymakers, we have focused on the ways that technology can power services and programs that benefit the communities where we live and all around the world. Between us we have been part of every stage of technology development—from design to testing to failure to trying again.

Although we are different people with different lived experiences, privileges, and perspectives, we share these same beliefs:

- Since humans create technology, it can't be neutral.
- Therefore, the opportunity and challenge is to more intentionally, inclusively, and collaboratively build the technologies that come next so they can support us in the bigger work of building an equitable world.
- The only way we can truly make this happen is to use models that are built on community-centered values.

We are practitioners, and we hope to always be. Every day we are in the practice of changing ourselves so that we can change the world. We invite you to be a practitioner too. That calls for always learning, testing, reflecting, and practicing the ways we can stretch ourselves and our teams and our systems to bend in new ways. This work can be started anywhere, in whatever space you are in today.

WHY THIS BOOK?

We did not want to make a "how to" book. We did not want to suggest that doing things differently—that changing organizations, funding institutions, and systems—is easy, or that there could be a checklist for making an equitable world. There's no easy way to change the systems and practices that have created the imperfect technologies we have today.

What we did want was to use the opportunity to write a book as a platform to uplift as many people as we can. We invite you to learn more about the work of those quoted and referenced throughout the following chapters.

Truly creating an equitable world will most certainly require contributions from everyone in some way. As this book is a practice in thinking about new options and priorities, we also want it to be a practice in looking for inspiration from a diversity of other efforts and acknowledging the lessons that many different people may offer us. There are so many more people, projects, organizations, and leaders that we wish we could have included, but we could never have made an exhaustive list.

Instead, we invite you to share, promote, and support the list of people and projects you know and have learned from in your work with others. We invite you to uplift folks in your community. Introduce them to others, recommend them for grants and investment, collaborate with them on new ideas, and invest in relationship-building—just for the sake of doing so. As everyone does this more and more, we will collectively accelerate the learning and new connections that can help us move forward.

WHO IS THIS BOOK ABOUT?

We focus on five key groups that for now we are identifying as follows: social impact organizations, technologists, funders, policymakers, and communities. And while we use these titles for the groups, we acknowledge that there are many different terms and titles in use for all of these groups, and that we have little language that feels comprehensively accurate. Our language is always evolving and we look forward to the emergence of better terms that more accurately reflect the realities for folks in these groups. And, part of our vision for what comes next is a world where these groups are not siloed or separated in the way they often are today. Belief systems about where resources are accumulated and how they are distributed, who has access to training and decision making, and what work is worthy of investment are core to what will be changed so that we can organize and collaborate in new ways. We need to shift how we make change, how we resource communities, and how we build tools. Doing so will help us let go of the language that doesn't serve us, and from that new reality will come better terms.

Social Impact Organizations: This is the most challenging term for us because it is so clearly inadequate to all that is accomplished by these organizations. Using a term like nonprofit, charity, or non-governmental organization (NGO) would have implied that we were focused on a specific country or culture. The term "social change" has different connotations for different communities, and "civil society" is used in varying ways. Though we could argue that every organization, technology, and product has an impact—positive or negative—we decided to use "social impact organizations" to refer to the diverse set of entities who operate with a social benefit mission. We know that US 501(c)(3) registered nonprofits are not the only ones who meet this definition; other entities such as associations, charities, NGOs, and even public benefit corporations may also be part of this work.

Technologists: We regularly talk about how, at this point in time, anyone could be considered a technologist. So it was naturally difficult for us to separate those creating software and applications from those with no coding experience who nonetheless use and manage technologies. In this book we use "technologists" to indicate those who develop technology—whether they do it in proprietary systems or open source; as a staff person of a social impact organization or a technology company; or as a purpose-built system for social impact or for the commercial market.

Funders: There are many terms for funders that are intended to mean many different things to different people. We did not want to write about only private philanthropy, venture capital, corporate social responsibility programs, or individual major donors. Our choice to use "funders" was to create an intentional umbrella over all of the ways that social impact work, community initiatives, and technology projects are and could be financially resourced.

Policymakers: Each of these terms is challenged by regional and geographic nomenclature, but perhaps none as much as "policymakers." In this book we talk about projects that may be on a

neighborhood scale or a global scale, so referring to mayors, coun-
selors, cabinet members, or anything else would inherently limit
how we discuss these ideas. Similarly, we want to open up space
in recognizing that not all policies are created by elected officials—
there are appointed officials, departments authorized to set policy,
and more. We use "policymakers" inclusively for all those in a
position to create policies that impact technology, social impact
work, and all of our communities.

Communities: What someone might mean when they use the word
"community" will vary by the person, their intention, and the
context of the conversation. Community is critically important to
what we talk about here, and what we mean by the word
"community" is often, if not always, subjective. Who is your
community? You likely have several: communities of shared identity, communities of place, communities of interest, and more.
No one has only one community; we hope you will keep in mind
the plurality of communities in and around all of us as you read
the following chapters.

These aforementioned groups and terms are separated for the sake
of direct discussion about opportunities and needs. Of course, a single
person could be represented by all five terms: someone who works in a
social impact organization as a technologist could receive a grant to
distribute funds, could educate a policymaker on the data from their
research, and then engage with their community to advocate for
change. We are, each of us, full and complex people—as you read, you
may find that you have been or are now part of each of these groups in
different ways and at different times. The fluidity of our lived experiences manifests in the ways we have, or have access to, power in some
of these groups but not others. We hope to shift toward a world that
doesn't create barriers between these groups. But even before that day,
today, together, we have all the resources we need to make any
world possible.

WHAT DO WE DREAM OF?

People sometimes think technology is the way to address inequality. We don't think that, and that's not what we suggest in this book. In fact, that's not what our decades of experience with myriad organizations across sectors has taught us. Technology is a tool and nothing more; it's people who have ideas and solutions. As Octavia Butler said, "There is no single answer that will solve all our future answers, there is no magic bullet, there are thousands of answers, and you could be one of them, if you choose to be."

In asking for you and others to dream and imagine something different from what we have today, we want to acknowledge the privilege that it is to have the space for that dreaming. We have that space because we don't need to figure out where we'll get our next meal or a bed, or find medicine or support, or access care or safety. So, that's what we dream of:

- That we all have space to rest.
- That we all have space to collaborate.
- That we all have space to build relationships.

We don't ask communities to do the labor to undo the oppressive systems around them. We dream about self-determination for communities and community members.

We don't want to perpetuate work that follows old expectations or dominant priorities. We dream about community-centered work that builds from community-centered values.

This book is an exercise in doing that dreaming. We ask questions to prompt your thinking even beyond what is written here. We need more imagination, and we need more people doing that imagining together.

Chapter One

Where We Are and How We Got Here

Technology. Just the word itself evokes a range of emotions and images.

For some, technology represents hopes and promises for innovations to simplify our lives and connect us to the people and issues we want to be connected to, almost as though technology is a collection of magical inventions that will serve the whims of humans. To others, technology represents expertise and impartial arbitration. In this case, people perceive that to create a solid technological solution one must be exceptionally smart. Technology, with this mindset, is also neutral, and therefore inherently good because it can focus on calculated efficiencies rather than human messiness. Others have heard that technologists "move fast and break things," or that progress is made "at the speed of technology"—and accordingly associate the word "technology" with speed and innovation constantly improving the world and forcing humans to keep up.

In contrast, the mention of "technology" fills some people with caution and trepidation. The word can conjure fears and concerns—fueled by movies and imaginations—of robots taking over the world and "evil" people turning technology against "good" people. Others are skeptical of how often technology is promised to solve all problems but ends up falling short—especially in the many ways it can exclude or even inflict physical, emotional, or mental harm. Unfortunately, there are many examples of technology making it more difficult for people to complete tasks, contributing to feelings of anxiety or depression, and causing physical strain in bodies. The potential for these and other harms are what cause some to be concerned or fearful about technology. And, for some, the mention of technology stokes fears of isolation: for those less comfortable with modern technology, the fear of being left out of conversations or of not being able to engage in the world pairs with the very practical isolation that lack of access can create.

Many people hold a number of these sometimes contradictory emotions and perspectives at the same time. In fact, individuals often define "technology" differently. Although some may think of technology as being exclusively digital programs or internet tools or personal computing devices, in this book we define "technology" in the broadest sense: digital systems as well as everything from smart fridges to phones to light systems in a building to robots and more.

WE LIVE IN A WORLD OF TECHNOLOGY

Regardless of how complicated feelings about tech may be, we all must embrace it: we live in the age of technology. Whether you consider how food travels from farms to tables, how clothes are manufactured, or even how we communicate, tech has changed and continues to change how these processes happen. Certainly, we complete a number of services through technology systems—shopping for clothes, ordering weeknight meals, scheduling babysitters, and applying for tax refunds. We expect the technology tools and applications we use to provide smooth and seamless experiences for us every time we use them. In many cases, with the exception of the occasional glitch or unavailable webpage, technology works how we expect it to; it helps us get things done.

Unfortunately, not everyone has the same experiences with technology. The late 1980s brought us the first commercially available automatic faucets, which promised relief for arthritic hands and a more sanitary process for all. Some people reported sporadic functioning, however; the faucets worked for some but not others. When the manufacturers researched the problem, an unexpected commonality appeared: the faucets didn't work for people with dark skin. In an engineering environment dominated by white developers, testers, and salesmen—and we deliberately choose the suffix "men"—people with dark skin had not been included among the test users. In a more recent example, in 2016 Microsoft launched @TayAndYou, a Twitter bot designed to learn from Twitter users and develop the ability to carry on Twitter conversations with users. Within one day, Microsoft canceled the program, because, as the *New York Times* stated, the bot "quickly became a racist jerk."[1]

In the name of efficiency and integrity, various technology systems are developed and implemented to monitor the distribution of social benefit programs. Organizer and academic Virginia Eubanks, who studies digital surveillance systems and the welfare system, has remarked that, for recipients of welfare programs, "technology is ubiquitous in their lives. But their interactions with it are pretty awful. It's exploitative and makes them feel more vulnerable."[2] Technology is used to automatically remove people who are legally entitled to services from systems that furnish government and NGO providers with data regarding the population that needs those services. In her book *Automating Inequality*, Eubanks describes a state-run health care benefits system that began automatically unenrolling members, and the associated volume of work individuals had to do to understand why they were, often wrongly, unenrolled and how to reenroll. It is also used to prevent someone from receiving services in one part of their lives because of a disputed interaction in a different part of their lives. In this case, notes on unsubstantiated reports of child abuse may remain in a parent's "file," and then used to cast suspicion on the adult if they seek additional support services. This is all tracked in the same government system.

"The technology has unintended consequences" is something many people in technology companies say when referring to products that don't work for a segment of the population, or to systems that leave people feeling exploited. However, these "unintended consequences" are often the same: they result in excluding or harming populations that have been historically ignored, historically marginalized, and historically underinvested in. The biases and systems that routinely exclude and oppress have spread from the physical world into the technological world.

How can we have these uneven, unequal experiences with technology when one of the supposed attributes of technology is impartiality? Isn't tech based on math and science and data—pure, immutable things that cannot change and therefore can be trusted? There are so many examples of how technology, regardless of how quickly it moved or innovated, repeatedly did not deliver on the hopes and promises for *all* people. Why?

We're not the first to ponder these questions. Many people, including ourselves, have concluded that technology is put into use by humans and, accordingly, is good or bad depending on the use case and context. Technology is also built by humans and, as a result, technology reflects the biases of its human creators. Melvin Kranzberg, a historian and former Georgia Tech professor of history of technology, in 1986, wrote about Six Laws of Technology, which acknowledge the partiality of technology within the context of society:[3]

1. Technology is neither good nor bad; nor is it neutral.
2. Invention is the mother of necessity.
3. Technology comes in packages, big and small.
4. Although technology might be a prime element in many public issues, nontechnical factors take precedence in technology-policy decisions.

5. All history is relevant, but the history of technology is the most relevant.
6. Technology is a very human activity—and so is the history of technology.

These laws are still applicable today. Technology, it turns out, is fairly useless on its own. High-speed trains would be irrelevant in a world without people or products to move. A beautifully designed shopping website is a waste if no one knows about or uses it. Technology exists within systems, within societies. The application of math and science, as well as the structure and collection of data, are all human inventions; they are all therefore constructed to conform to the many rules, assumptions, and hierarchies that systems and societies have created. These supposedly impartial things, then, are actually the codification of the feelings, opinions, and thoughts of the people who created them. And, historically, the people who create the most ubiquitous technology are a small subset of the population who happen to hold a lot of power—whether or not they reflect the interests and feelings, opinions, and thoughts of the majority, let alone of the vulnerable.

IDA B WELLS Just Data Lab founder and author of the book *Race After Technology*, Princeton University Professor Ruha Benjamin takes it a step further. Because technology and systems are often built on these biased assumptions, "Sometimes, the more intelligent machine learning becomes, the more discriminatory it can be."[4]

What constitutes "technology" has evolved over time. Roughly shaped knives and stones used as hammers are widely considered the first technological inventions.[5] Fast-forward several millennia to the creation of a primitive internet. What started as a way for government researchers to share information across locations and across computers grew into the Advanced Research Projects Agency Network in the 1960s. From there, additional large and well-funded institutions, such as universities, created their own networks for researchers to share information. Next, mainframes—large computers used by companies for centralized data processing—became popular. With the creation of a standard communication protocol for computers on any network to use, the internet was born in 1983.

Since then, the pace of technology development has only accelerated. The spread of personal computers and distributed computing meant that more individuals outside of institutional environments had access to technology and to information. People quickly created businesses, shared ideas, and communicated with others through the "dot-com" boom of the 1990s. We have more recently seen the rise of cloud computing, on-demand availability of computing power, and big data—the large amount of complex data that organizations collect. Techniques to process this data, learn from it, and make predictions based on it are known as data science, machine learning, and artificial intelligence. As a result, we now have a world where many people have access to a tremendous amount of computing power in the palm of their hands; companies can understand exactly what people want and create new content that meets those desires; and people can envision technology touching, and improving, every aspect of their lives.

In less than a century, we have gone from creating the internet to sending people to the moon with mainframe technology to building smartphones with more computing power than what was used to send people to the moon. And as technology has evolved, so evolve those who develop the technology—the "technologists." Unfortunately, whereas technological developments increase the percentage of the population who can engage with it, the diversity of technologists has decreased. The large tech companies are overwhelmingly filled with people who identify as white and male, despite the reality that this group doesn't comprise the majority percentage of humans on earth. But the technology field hasn't always been this way. The movie *Hidden Figures*, based on the book by Margot Lee Shetterly, told the story of the African American women of West Area Computers—a division of NACA, the precursor of NASA—who helped propel the space race by being "human computers" manually analyzing data and creating data visualizations. US Navy Rear Admiral Grace Hopper invented the first computer compiler, a program that transforms written human instructions into the format that computers can read directly; this led to her cocreating COBOL, one of the earliest computing languages. Astonishingly, the percentage of women studying computer science peaked in the mid-1980s. We know, intuitively, that talent is evenly distributed around the world, and yet an enduring perception in tech is that the Silicon Valley model is the epitome of success. The Silicon Valley archetype, in addition to still being predominantly white and male, also privileges individuals who can devote the majority of their waking hours to their tech jobs—and who care more about moving fast than about breaking things. The archetype emphasizes making the world conform to their expectations, rather than using the world's realities to shape and mold their own products. And with a purported state of the world being defined by a smaller proportion of the population, the technology being constructed creates an ideal world for only a limited, privileged few.

TECHNOLOGY TO SUPPORT SOCIAL CHANGE

It's against a backdrop of all of these factors—the complicated and sometimes inaccurate feelings about technology, the significant benefit that technology can provide, the reality that technology isn't neutral— that conversations about tech created for and in the social impact sector begin.

For the purposes of this book, we define the "social impact sector" as the not-for-profit ecosystem—including NGOs (nongovernmental organizations) and mutual aid organizations and community organizers—that promotes social or political change, often by delivering services to target populations in order to both improve communities and strengthen connections within societies. As the name implies, organizations in the social impact sector don't make a profit, but rather apply all earned and donated funds to the pursuit of their mission. Social impact sector organizations can vary in size and scope, from a few people in one location to thousands of people around the world. A common aspect of these mission-driven organizations is that they focus on the mission first—feeding hungry children, promoting sustainable farming, delivering health care equitably, and more.

Often, practitioners start and lead these organizations because of their knowledge of the social or political issue and their ability to deploy resources to make an impact. This focus on serving the defined clients, combined with the pressure to show that the funds received are directly affecting those who need the support, rather than being allocated to cover administrative overhead, the category that technology services often fall into. The technical and interconnected world in which we live, however, requires that to remain relevant and effective, the social impact sector must embrace technology to deliver its services—a necessity that has existed for quite some time. But given the global phenomenon of COVID-19 and what it has wreaked, the challenges of operating, organizing, and delivering services during a pandemic have revealed that, in terms of what needs to happen now in the social impact sector, and certainly what comes next, technology must be deeply integrated into how these organizations conduct business.

One of the many ways the pandemic has stressed our society is in significantly changing people's economic status. Although some have profited as the virus and its variants have spread and claimed lives across the globe, many, many more have lost not just accumulated wealth but also vital income. Service providers have struggled to keep up with the vast increase of those in need. And we will not quickly recover; it is predicted that a number of nonprofits will no longer exist five years after the worst of the pandemic has passed. Nonprofits have no choice but to be more efficient.

But the onus isn't solely on the social impact organizations themselves; many technologists have not considered the social impact sector an applicable setting for their talents. Fewer are inspired to take the time and care to advance complicated social issues for the benefit of one's fellow humans, and even fewer actively work to minimize any harm to individuals that the technology could cause. And, even when technologists do want to support the social impact sector, they often don't know how to support it in helpful ways. As Meredith Broussard wrote in her book *Artificial Unintelligence*, "There has never been and never will be a technological innovation that moves us away from human nature."[6] The social impact sector reminds us that human nature is to live in community.

When we unpack what it means to be a technologist in the social impact sector, we have to start with the basics. We must understand that technology in social impact organizations is expansive. It includes IT systems, management systems, and products to help the organization deliver services to its clients and supporters. IT systems include tech such as broadband internet, computers and mobile devices, printers, and computing power. Management systems include donor databases, impact tracking systems, performance dashboards, and customer relationship management systems. Products that support service delivery could include a custom-built website to allow people to schedule visits with a caseworker, a route-optimization tool that plans the most efficient delivery routes, algorithms to ensure data integrity in training software, or a tool that processes and presents data to inform policymakers as they legislate. As you can see, this breadth of technology requires a variety of different skills to execute. Add to which—given that the social impact sector exists to improve lives, the security and privacy that organizations implement in their program designs need to be considered in every aspect of the technology design.

The significant issues the social impact sector tackles, combined with the logistical challenges of reaching people in locations far and wide, requires deep technical expertise and sophisticated design. As this has not been readily available, social impact sector organizations have deprioritized and deemphasized technology for decades. But the current climate is such that those organizations must have technology appropriate to their context, even if it isn't the fanciest technology. This can be a significant challenge—good and bad—for "expert" technologists who are used to entering new environments as tech saviors with an understanding that their expertise will immediately translate into a new space. When speed and immediate contributions are prioritized, the work needed to prevent harmful unintended consequences is often neglected. There is no space for the "tech savior" mindset in the social impact sector, nor for technologists inclined to quickly jump into developing tech because they've developed tech elsewhere. The social impact sector has its own expertise—and, while technical skills are transferable, understanding of social problems and community contexts is not. Even within the social impact sector, "design with, not for" has been a mantra of the civic tech world for years, but this idea alone is insufficient. Designing with, not for does not transfer ownership of information and solutions; long-term ownership, with the ability to modify, expand, or turn off the solutions, is necessary for communities to maintain their own power.

The recognition that expertise does not magically transfer between sectors is only one of the design constraints for developing technology within the social impact sector. Though the sector benefits from government funding, it relies primarily on philanthropic funding. As a result, technology budgets in the social impact sector are perennially tight, leaving tough decisions about whether to develop a more costly custom solution that meets and respects client needs or buy a ready-made, imperfect solution that reaches more clients. When assessing off-the-shelf technology, social impact sector leaders recognize that deploying technology that has a track record of marginalizing and disenfranchising people—such as video conferencing software without closed captioning, making it difficult to use by the Deaf community—will not work for organizations that serve historically marginalized and disenfranchised populations. In addition, because these organizations often deal with different populations with immediate needs, they don't have the luxury of adopting an "if you build it they will come" mindset, or of deploying a solution that benefits only a portion of their clients simply because it was too difficult to develop something for everyone.

Even once all these factors are addressed, organizations then need to figure out what should happen next. How do they plan for and carry out system maintenance and upgrades? Is what was done relevant only to the particular organization, or is it something that others in the social impact sector can also benefit from? Given their mission-driven nature, many organizations turn their focus back to their direct clients before answering these questions. The "technology versus client support" consideration is a false dichotomy, but it is one that many social impact sector organizations feel nonetheless.

This Is Where We Are

Figure 1.1 illustrates the factors today that don't serve us; it depicts the current state of systemic exclusion. Most resources are difficult to access, as though behind a fence. Even if a person is able to gain entry to the general location with resources, for the average individual, the resources are siloed—people and functions and services happen separately and without coordination. If someone is not already in a silo, they encounter systems of control and are denied entry to exclusive, elite spaces.

The themes present in this illustration—exclusive access, systems of control, and centralized power structures—reflect some of the challenges outlined in this chapter. In addition, the technology present in the figure has been discarded; the technology that was perhaps useful in some contexts has been cast aside and is now not able to serve anyone. Finally, the illustration doesn't show anything growing. With pollution in the background, the emphasis is on seeing buildings and structures, rather than on including people. Throughout this book, we invite you to look for these themes and barriers in the chapters as we discuss opportunities for change.

Figure 1.1   Current State: Systemic Exclusion

Social impact sector organizations work hard every day to push back against the inequities and injustices in society. With limited budgets they manage to effect real, positive change on a number of social issues and improve the quality of life for many humans; however, this is done in a world where resources are difficult to access and coordinate. We often assume that the oppressive systems will always continue to exist, and will even strengthen. But what if this weren't the case? What if we could restructure how we think about developing systems and services to move beyond this picture and truly exist in a world where humans are centered and justice is pursued? We must consider how the different levers in society can work together; we must consider how we build the tech that comes next.

Chapter Two
Where Are We Going?

We are writing this book while the COVID-19 global pandemic rages on, while protests and legislation related to racial equity continue in the streets and in city halls—and every aspect of our lives grows more dependent on technology every day. Living within these realities, what do we see?

Technology companies have pledged to diversify their staff amid various campaigns calling for them to disclose the racial makeup of their management and leadership teams. During the first few months of the pandemic in 2020, many of those same companies offered their products at free or newly discounted options to nonprofits or even individuals. Of course, most had fine print specifying these offers weren't permanent.

The philanthropic sector is full of pledges and commitment statements about everything from addressing racial inequity to making their grantmaking more accessible and less onerous. Such assistance is indeed helpful to social impact organizations, local mutual aid efforts, and every kind of community institution, all of whom have struggled to address skyrocketing needs for critical services and programs with greatly depleted human and financial resources. In the summer of

2020, Deloitte's Monitor Institute reported an estimated 10–40% contraction in the US nonprofit sector with one out of every three organizations already closed or at risk of doing so.[1]

Such pledges and commitments by technology providers and philanthropy are important in many ways, but they are not enough to help many organizations and communities even to stay afloat—let alone to build a better world.

As we discussed in chapter 1, the systems and challenges around us—the same systems that created the need for an entire social impact sector to provide lifesaving and enriching programs—have also deeply influenced the technology systems, tools, and culture present in our work and lives. We cannot build a better world through only more nonprofits or more inclusive services. If the technology-enabled systems, data collection, and even service models we employ toward a positive mission are themselves causing harm, because they are extractive, don't acknowledge our identities, or are inaccessible, we must acknowledge that harm and make change—in both the technology tools themselves and in the way we create technology for our needs.

An equitable world will require change from every one of us, as individuals and organizations and sectors and communities. Critical in this is changing our relationship with technology generally and changing the technologies we have available so that more appropriate, relevant, and equitable technology is available to meet our needs. Even more critical is practicing the big work of envisioning that we can do things differently.

Let's think for a moment about social impact work as building a house. We don't start by pulling up plans for each tool; we have a blueprint of the house and financial estimates for all the permits, materials, and labor that will be needed through to completion. We don't focus on how many saws and nail guns we have, nor do we expect that the full house can be built using only a hammer.

Similarly, we need to ensure that our relationship to technology, as individuals and as organizations, is one that acknowledges digital tools are just that: tools. Despite the efforts of Silicon Valley to frame every application and service as comprehensive "solutions," these digital tools need to be considered with appropriate expectations for what they can actually do and what they can't. Staying focused, instead, on the goal we have ahead will enable us to select the best tools as and when needed. Keeping our community central in our processes, through engaging many people in the goal setting, decision making, design, and implementation of our work, allows us also to be accountable for technology use that causes harm and to make appropriate adjustments. To return to the house-building analogy, if we selected tools that caused avoidable accidents, we need to find alternative ways to meet our goal without endangering our laborers.

As we build toward a better world, those putting technology to work need to be in control of the technology we choose and how it works for us, not the other way around.

OUR VISION

An equitable world is one where everyone has access to affordable, healthy food, a secure place to live, and the freedom and safety to pursue a life filled with loving relationships, joy, expression, and learning. Equitable technology includes the networks, hardware, software, and services that support everyone's access to, participation in, and fulfillment in an equitable world. Technology is integral to how we live our lives today, from registering for social services to accessing health care and from pursuing education to communicating with family, but to achieve an equitable world, our relationship to technology will need to be different from what it is today. Fortunately, the technologies we now have can be replaced by ones made in more equitable ways.

As tempting as it is to focus only on the image of that better world, we need to focus on how to create the bridge for all of us to get there. One of the lessons we can draw from how technology serves—or doesn't serve—the world today is that how you develop technology is as important as what technology you develop.

Social Impact Organizations

It is likely that employees, volunteers, board members, or others who are part of a social impact organization with a mission to do good— whether through direct service or not, on a local scale or a global one— believe that the work of the organization matters. Many communities are supported through a diversity of valuable social impact organizations, from food pantries and book banks to concerts in the park, and advocacy efforts to shift local policies to advocating for the rights of community groups. These missions are all important pieces of the fabric of programs, services, and support that have direct impact on communities everywhere. The best way to further the value of these missions and programs is to ensure that the administration and delivery of the work is advancing the mission, too—and not inadvertently contributing to the issues the mission aims to address.

Technology is a big part of this unintended negative contribution— from extractive data collection to perpetuating digital exclusion. And those working in social impact organizations are in a critical position to catalyze change for the way technology is selected, implemented, budgeted, planned, and used toward the mission.

For technology to work for us, we don't need everyone to get a degree in computer science or learn to code—we don't have to all become highly trained technologists for technology to be successful. It's critical that we all actively engage with people who approach shared problems from different angles and perspectives. We need people who are experts in their missions and community's needs to collaborate with us on the many challenges we face. Leading practitioners in particular are well positioned to ask important questions, require processes for selecting and using technology that best meet the mission, and connect the opportunities of technology systems to the important impact they want to achieve.

Our vision is for technology projects, funders, and policymakers to prioritize the participation and perspective of communities most affected by the many intersecting systems we're working to change.

Funders and Investors

All those who are part of the funding mechanisms of social impact and technology—be that private philanthropy, corporate philanthropy, venture capital, individual donors, or other financial resourcing models—are in a critical position to shift these systems and sectors toward change. In order to meet the missions of social impact organizations, as well as the needs of our communities, the resourcing for that work must change in a number of important ways.

Like those working in social impact organizations, funders of all types must understand how the emergence of their roles and sectors exist only because of the same systems that created the community's needs in the first place. Capitalism, white supremacy, and other extractive systems of power perpetuate inequitable realities. Together, we need to fundamentally shift how we resource projects, organizations, and technology development in order to produce different outcomes.

In many of the existing funding dynamics for social impact work and for technology development, the power and focus are on the funders, who can decide if or how a project moves forward. This dynamic needs to be reversed so that the communities and people receiving the social impact work and technology can be the ones setting the priorities. We can't continue to perpetuate the belief that those with the most money know best; instead, we need funders and investors who believe that the resourcing they bring to a project is in service to the knowledge, lived experience, and vision of those doing the work and those for whom the work is designed to serve. Along with this belief comes the reminder that supporting social impact work and technology development requires resourcing that is not exclusively financial. Many funders, regardless of their type or size or investment area, have access to power, relationships, capital, services, and infra-structure that can all be leveraged toward the goal.

Our vision is for resources to be managed and prioritized by com-munities and organizations putting technology to use for positive impact, so that their needs and realities are centered in development, instead of on the priorities of those with the most financial assets.

Technology Creators and Providers

Technology creators or service providers are positioned at the crux of significant power and responsibility.

In our world of accelerating digital connections, communication, and information sharing, technology creators and providers hold many of the keys to unlock what we can do today and where we might go tomorrow. Critical to unlocking opportunities is recognizing that tech-nology is not neutral. Technology tools—data management systems or social media, accounting tools or artificial intelligence—cannot be neutral, because humans created them. The cumulative biases, beliefs, lived experiences, and understanding of those creators naturally guide and limit how they imagine a potential solution, as well as how they design technology to deliver it.

We don't even necessarily need *neutral* technology. But we do need to reconsider who a technologist is or could be, how and where tech-nology is created, and what our technology providers could do to be accountable for the full impact of their products.

Our vision is for those who stand to be most affected are brought into the process to give perspective and experience in the development of technology, with a deep understanding of the real-world use cases for users prioritized over profit.

Policymakers

Those who make policies about the ways technology is built, funded, or used essentially design guardrails and checkpoints. It is important that they have a complete understanding of community context, access, and implications of technology. Do the policies prioritize safety and minimize harm? Or do they favor those with the privileges of knowledge, access, and resources, forcing everyone else to wait?

The laws, policies, and regulations for the internet and digital tools that get made today will either accelerate or hinder the efforts of other groups working for change, including social impact organizations, funders, and technology providers. Regulation and requirements around our digital infrastructure can't be thought of as something with clear geographic boundaries or as something constrained by financial penalty. Our digital infrastructure will only become more global; the systems for designing and enforcing policies for that infrastructure need to be global, too.

As noted earlier, the outcomes for policy work will be most successful when those potentially most affected are brought into the process to offer their perspective and experience. When communities who have been harmed by the technology tools and associated legal policies around them are able to convey their experience—not just once but repeatedly, in regular communication—the clarified need can influence the necessary improvements.

Our vision is that all policymaking concerning technology be designed with awareness of the full, continuing impact of that technology on its end users. Such accountability for impact, harm, and repair can most directly produce viable outcomes.

TECHNOLOGY THAT IS ACCOUNTABLE TO COMMUNITY

Ultimately, the fetishization and veneration of technology, especially the newest and shiniest of technologies, isn't sustainable—or even accessible—for many people. What is sustainable is values alignment, deep investment, and thoughtful planning. If we can commit to the work of realigning these values in ourselves, our organizations, and the world around us as part of the work toward any other social mission or cause, we could more readily build new, different, and equitable technology.

Our relationship to technology, largely created for and by the most privileged communities in our world, is a core component of the dismantling work necessary at all levels. We will not meet our missions and heal the societal harms our work addresses without a readiness to establish a practice of changing how we think about, use, create, invest in, and implement technology within our work.

What We Value

We can't expect different results without changing the way our social impact efforts, technology development, funding, and policymaking begin: with what we value. Here is where we start:

- An equitable world requires that we value the knowledge and wisdom of lived experience. The most affected individuals and communities need to be central to decisions about solutions and priorities.
- An equitable world requires that we value the participation of a diversity of people in decision making, planning, and building technology—regardless of their technical knowledge or training.
- An equitable world requires that we value accessibility as a priority from the start in all technology and social impact work.
- An equitable world requires that we value the multiple ways that change is made, balancing the need to meet immediate challenges with a long view for how we can systemically eliminate those challenges.
- An equitable world requires that we value the strength of collectively creating a vision of a better world. No single voice, visionary, or author of a future will work for everyone.

- An equitable world requires that we value the dedication of individuals and communities in pursuing knowledge, experience, and skills. A diversity of people with deep training and practice offers valuable resources in collective efforts for change.

None of this is new, and yet all of it is new. So many people have yearned for a different world—a freer world—in so many definitions of that idea. Many leaders, community organizers, developers, designers, and laborers have pushed for change in their fields and in their communities. Though progress has been made, some obstacles still feel insurmountable, and in many ways what to try next can feel equally unknowable.

But if we orient our compass by the values listed here, even though we don't know what the path ahead will look like, or even what the final destination will be, we can trust that we are headed in the right direction—because we are focused on inclusion, accessibility, and accountability to each other.

This Is Where We're Going

Although we don't know exactly what a world with these values will look like, we can start putting together a basic idea, especially in contrast to Figure 1.1 about the systemic exclusion where we are today. Figure 2.1, *Future State*, instead imagines some of the components of a more equitable world we are building toward.

The first important difference with this illustration of systemic inclusion, as compared with that of systemic exclusion in chapter 1, is that people are not only present but active participants shaping and enjoying their lives. There is space for connection and collaboration; there are resources available for everyone to share. Sustainability and justice feel accessible to everyone, with relationships and accountability

Figure 2.1   Future State: Systemic Inclusion

serving to support and protect individuals and the community. Ultimately, this is a world where people and the earth are thriving, joy and rest are plentiful, and growth is celebrated.

These themes and values are present throughout the following chapters in myriad ways—from the case studies to the new models for making change. There are many more situations and considerations that could be added to this illustration, but our hope is that this is a visualization that supports reflection and imagination. Identifying where more ideas could be added to this illustration is itself practice in pushing our minds to more and better realities. On the right side of the illustration there's a bridge leading somewhere beyond the page, which signifies our goal that the conversations and efforts that we individually and collectively take after reading this book will help build a bridge to what comes next. As we make progress in the long journey of changing our world, this illustration can be replaced by new ones that bring us closer and closer to a world that works for all of us.

WHAT WILL IT TAKE TO GET THERE?

This is a book about technology. This is a book about equity. This is a book about how we can meet community needs. More than anything, this is a book that asks you to ask questions, that invites you to join us in stretching our imaginations so that we can more readily embrace inclusion, accessibility, and accountability, and thus work more intentionally toward a world that works for all of us.

So how do we get there? The following chapters focus on different parts of the whole, including: the ways technology is used for social impact, how technologies are developed, opportunities for funding technology use and creation, changing the processes for designing and managing policies, and the various ways certain communities are excluded from accessing these spaces. These chapters also explore how we can change each of those pieces to instead prioritize the needs of affected communities, to build accountability around that impact, and to divest from old systems and patterns that do not serve equitable outcomes.

In chapter 3, we look at the way Rescuing Leftover Cuisine invested in technology to increase their impact and even scale the organization. This chapter is focused on technology used in and developed for social impact organizations, including technology culture and leadership development, as well as technology systems and investments.

In chapter 4, we learn about a technology project at John Jay College to better identify students at most risk of not graduating so that they can be connected to appropriate services. This chapter addresses technology development, both inside social impact organizations and for use by social change efforts, from the process of development and who is included to the ethics of developing technology today.

In chapter 5, our case study profiles the intentional prioritization Okta had on giving back to the sector and the formation of Okta for Good. This chapter covers how social impact work and social impact technology are funded through philanthropy, venture capital, and more. We discuss the way financial assets can be better directed into social change and how investments in technology are ultimately investments in communities.

In chapter 6, there are two case studies profiling the Rural Community Assistance Partnership and the National Digital Inclusion Alliance. This is the policymaking chapter but, importantly, we consider both policies that are made about technology and opportunities for that work to better engage communities, as well as how technology is used to support policymaking—all at the local, regional, national, and global levels.

In chapter 7, we spotlight the work of Atutu through the Project Sunbird initiative in Myanmar as an exemplary example of community-centered work. In this chapter, we focus on what may be required or valuable to enable communities to engage with the groups previously covered in chapters 3 through 6, including internet access, training, and social infrastructure.

Each of these chapters includes a Case Study to offer an in-depth exploration of a diversity of organizations and models already underway. These case studies each include direct quotes from someone involved in the profiled project, but it is important to acknowledge that each of these projects involved many more people in the past, today, and will include others in the future. Though they may not be quoted and named in the chapter, we are grateful for their leadership and contributions.

At the end of each of these chapters are Questions for What's Next. These are questions to ask ourselves and others to open up our imaginations to what is possible, to challenge assumptions and existing systems, and to bring us into closer relationships across these various sectors.

In chapters 8 and 9, we reflect on the five previous chapters and connect the themes, opportunities, and needs between them. Where we will go and what we will build next will be influenced by what we choose to value and how we enable collective changemaking, technology development, funding, and policymaking.

In chapter 10, we provide resources to support you starting conversations about this book with those you work or organize with, including discussion questions for reflection as well as an aggregation of the questions from within the chapters throughout the book.

We have identified throughout this book a variety of actions you can take to further this vision. But our biggest ask is this:

Whoever you are, wherever you are, you are part of this work. Start imagining something new today.

Chapter Three
Changing Technology Culture and Investments Inside Social Impact Organizations

Technology can accelerate the work of social change. It can also disrupt progress, exacerbate harms, and reinforce barriers. For technology to contribute meaningfully to the work of building a better world, social impact organizations need a cultural understanding of tech that keeps the focus on the mission and community—not on the tools themselves. They also need to invest strategically to meet that mission.

Technology changes every day—not just new apps on the market, but also updates to the tech you already use. Phones ping with application update notifications; sign-ups are tracked with a new event registration platform; an organization pilots a new customer service chatbot while their affiliate branch tests an SMS messaging service. With technology permeating most areas of life, organizations need to be intentional about how they adopt technology. Do staff and program participants, as well as the community at large, have the training and skills to keep up with the changes? Do organizations have the budgets to invest in technology best suited for community needs? For many employees of social impact organizations, the most pressing question is: How do I use technology to help me do my job more effectively, more efficiently?

Technology isn't going to solve everything—or anything—for us, but we certainly won't get far without it either. Shifting both the culture and investments around technology in social impact work starts with acknowledging that both people and technology are necessary—but one is not a replacement for the other. Technology should help with readily automated, routine tasks, allowing people to focus on the many things that require a human's focus. For example, processing participant data and populating data across systems can be managed by a database and integrations with it—whereas, analyzing that data for trends or areas to explore should be handled by staff who are cognizant of both the context of the data and the goals for the participants.

But this isn't to say that tech is always great and should be used— and the mission and programs need to fit around the available technology. Technology can best be used in service to a mission and community when processes and tools are built to meet the needs of users and participants. People need to come first, not the tools.

CASE STUDY: RESCUING LEFTOVER CUISINE

Technology platforms and systems can accelerate a small team's progress and increase the scale of an organization's social impact. Technology's critical role in increasing social impact has proven true at Rescuing Leftover Cuisine (RLC) since 2013.

Robert Lee cofounded the nonprofit organization Rescuing Leftover Cuisine in New York City in 2013, and became the full-time CEO in 2014. The mission of RLC is to provide solutions to prevent excess wholesome cuisine from being wasted, which they facilitate locally by helping businesses, kitchens, and other food donors who have extra food donate it to nonprofit human service agencies that distribute it to food-insecure communities. Robert, a child of Korean immigrant parents, understood the need to prevent food waste from an early age as his family experienced food insecurity and worked to make sure nothing brought home was wasted. From this firsthand experience, Robert knew that he wanted to prevent his family from facing that struggle again.

RLC started out like many organizations do, at a very small human scale. Recruiting and managing the food donor partners and human service agency recipients took place through phone calls and emails. Volunteers picked up and delivered donated food mostly on foot. Communication and inventory, tracking and evaluation were all managed through almost entirely manual systems. As a team of three, the organization's technology infrastructure was created through pro bono volunteers, interns, and other volunteers creating an ad hoc suite of tools that did not integrate with each other and led to disjointed experiences for community members. Volunteers looking to sign up to bring donations from a restaurant to a community center needed to review an online calendar to find available spots, but had to contact RLC staff via email to sign up for the event. Despite the awkwardness of the platforms in place, the organization was succeeding: food was saved, people were fed. It was valuable, important work.

After a few years of operations and local growth in NYC, it was clear that in order to really expand their reach and impact, RLC needed better technology systems, especially those that made for more streamlined experiences and enabled the community—whether food donors, agency recipients, or volunteers—to do more themselves on the website, thus relieving the heavy burden on staff time to coordinate everything. Because the small team did not have technical expertise internally, they partnered with Chris La Pilusa of Calliope Consulting to start working on technical strategy and platform development. This partnership was more than a one-time outsourced technology project; it was a long-term commitment to balancing immediate improvements with bigger platform vision. "RLC was looking for a tech partner who understood nonprofits while professionally holding deadlines and communicating effectively," explains Robert. "The unique challenges we faced and the solutions we needed were complicated and nuanced. We sought to find a true partner who was able to help us navigate these challenges."

First on the list to address was reducing the administrative overhead required by RLC's staff, as Chris explains:

> When we first engaged with RLC, it was important to gain a deep understanding of their operations, and find where we could augment their mission with better technology solutions. We met with RLC's staff and reviewed how they conducted business both offline and through their website. It was important to instill a sense of what was possible with better approaches, and engage the imagination to deliver tools that would streamline and automate their processes. Together, we progressively laid a roadmap that would address immediate needs and build foundational features that could continue to be built upon and enhanced into the future.

Community feedback has been core to the development process for four years now, from the internal community of staff and the outside community groups of the food donors, the human service agency recipients, and the volunteers who connect the food donations between the two. RLC uses a Trello board for development requests, a project management tool that allows for columns of categorized content with drag-and-drop boxes users can move between columns and directly add reactions and comments. All requests for new features or technical changes are added to the board in the Requests column where feedback from the community and staff rank the ideas with the most critical and requested options moving over into the queue for development.

Then, after implementation and testing, they are moved into the Completed column.

"Opening the floor for all internal team members to share their ideas and weigh in on their needs using the Trello platform has allowed us to be much more transparent, intentional, and inclusive about our website's continued development," explains Catherine Smiley, Chief Operating Officer at RLC. "It also helps us to ensure that we're developing areas of actual need rather than what we perceive to be priorities."

Building a purpose-built platform to facilitate many of the day-to-day components of the donation processes has had many valuable outcomes for RLC. First, moving many of the tactical coordination and scheduling tasks off of staff and into automated systems or tools that the donors, recipients, and volunteers could manage themselves meant that the roles of the small staff could shift into more strategic positions. "As we were able to automate more and more manual work through the development of the RLC website, we were able both to rework the organization's structure by consolidating what was previously the work of several people into one operations role and hire for new roles with an increased focus on strategy and expansion," said Catherine.

Shifting the staff roles as the organization's technology systems enabled more strategic thinking also meant intentionally shifting the organization's culture around technology. "As opposed to dictating how new technology initiatives would look and feel, it was important to instill a sense of collaboration, where RLC would feel free to explain their needs, and Calliope could propose different ideas and alternatives for implementation," Chris reflects. "These conversations would lead to ideation amongst the RLC team and spark new concepts and alternatives for what the technology platform could do. This approach has allowed RLC to gain a greater perspective into what is possible and how to strategically approach their software development investments."

Collaboration is important between RLC and Calliope as the technology partner.

> RLC has the primary voice in determining their priorities and vision, and we meet for monthly planning sessions to determine what will be worked on and when. New features and enhancements are discussed and prioritized based on feasibility and estimated time commitment. Calliope provides the designs and workflows for review and feedback from RLC, so there is a clear understanding of what is being delivered and how it will work. Progress and status updates are regularly shared in weekly meetings, to ensure there is consistent and clear communication on both sides. The RLC Board of Directors also has a designated group committed to guiding and overseeing technology outcomes. We schedule monthly meetings to discuss higher level strategic goals and ensure that we are investing our time efficiently and effectively. This full participation from all levels within the organization from inception to execution helps make the relationship successful.

A focus on the strategic technology plans for RLC has enabled them to expand to more cities, facilitate more donations, and ultimately feed more people. RLC's work isn't about technology, but smart technology investments have enabled them to continue increasing their impact. Today, RLC has expanded beyond New York City and is now operating in eight locations around the United States.

"Our investments in technology have totally transformed our operations and allowed us to increase our impact but we know our website will never be 'finished,'" says Catherine. "We're constantly making improvements and building new functionality with a focus on creating a smooth, streamlined, and engaging experience for our rescuers. RLC has ambitious goals for growth and expansion and we are relying heavily on our technology to achieve those goals."

RLC is not an organization with a technology-focused mission. But strategic and intentional technology investments have enabled the impact of their mission to grow faster and wider than ever possible without it. Community input—from staff to rescuers to donors—has informed every iteration of their technology platforms, connecting technology priorities to program priorities each step of the way.

INSIDE THE PRACTICE OF CHANGE

What technologies have been available, and how they've been put to use, has been heavily researched and analyzed both inside and outside the tech sector. Since 2005, NTEN has conducted research in particular on the ways social impact organizations in the United States and beyond budget, staff, train, and utilize technology. Those methods have shifted dramatically over the last few decades. In the 1990s and early 2000s, organizations focused on technical capacity grants and initiatives that brought in actual computers or set up direct internet access—essentially the nuts and bolts and connectivity. Once those were established, tech funding expanded to setting up core systems like a database and a website. Over time, more systems became understood as critical for an organization, including mass messaging tools, program and project management, and even social media. One consistent finding in NTEN's research over the years is that staff in organizations report having the technology to do their work, but not the training and knowledge to put it to work—they don't necessarily always need more or different tools, but skill building to use what they have in better ways.

Among the most compelling trends NTEN's 15 years of research has uncovered is how sometimes a social impact organization's technology adoption does not correlate with its effectiveness. Regarding budget size and staff size, bigger is not necessarily better. Simply spending more—but on the wrong things or in wasteful ways—doesn't automatically make an organization more effective; similarly, having specific tools or products doesn't make an organization more likely to meet its mission. (This assessment doesn't apply for organizations at the extremes of the spectrum as there will need to be some budget, and some people, and some technology.)

So, what are the factors that do influence an organization's technology effectiveness? Technology decision making, budgeting, and planning. That means there's real opportunity for every social impact organization to use technology strategically to increase their impact in their mission and community—as long as they're intentional regarding the budget and staffing they have. So before we consider how to select the best technology for an organization, we'll first focus on establishing a viable culture for that technology.

Tech Culture and Leadership

We've all heard the tropes foisted upon the social impact sector: this work is for charity; it shouldn't be paid or professionalized; it is work of the heart, and not a place for sophisticated strategies and innovation. These assertions are absolutely untrue. In addition, articles and think pieces regularly contend that the social impact sector isn't "keeping pace" with the corporate world's approaches, that it "lags behind" in adopting models from the for-profit world, and that the "disrupters" or "innovators" in social impact are those that come from other industries. Unfortunately, staff, volunteers, board members, and program participants or service beneficiaries collectively buy into both sets of thinking, which just perpetuates starvation cycles for social impact funding and training.

Changing how social impact teams think about technology can also improve many other important aspects of the work, including staff roles and advancement, training and professionalization, program effectiveness and community impact, and values and trust in both the mission and community. Investing in technology really means investing in people, focusing on the community, and planning for processes that allow for participation and collaboration across teams.

Invest in Technology for All Staff   At this point in the development of our technical world and organizational realities, every person in an organization uses technology. Technology is not solely used by those with "IT" or "technology" in their job title, nor is tech exclusively the database or the phone system. Technology is the tools and systems as well as the ways we put them to work. And if technology is being used by every staff person, it should be acknowledged in their job description, in how they are evaluated, in how they are trained, and in the professional development they have access to.

First is the consideration for how technology is included in job postings. Unfortunately, many organizations often do this by listing requirements or expectations for candidates having experience using the exact suite of systems and applications currently in use in the organization. Requiring applicants to have specific technology experiences realistically means only individuals with the privilege to have already had access to the same technologies at previous jobs, with the added privilege of having those jobs in organizations that adequately supported staff training. Instead of further maintaining inequitable access to positions in social impact organizations, requirements for applicants should be about eagerness to use technology and experience learning new things.

Once an applicant is hired, the practice of naming technology in their job description informs how and where they make decisions about technology as well as what support and training they will need. Including this clarity around technology management in every staff person's job description requires that managers and technology-responsible staff acknowledge the roles, responsibilities, and authority around the technology decisions and use that are granted to each member of the team, something that will determine the organization's culture around technology. This is not to say that every job description should include the same parameters for technology, but that whatever those parameters are should be clearly articulated for each position. As such, every new hire's orientation and training can be guided by the technology-related responsibilities in their job description, which ensures a closer alignment to needs and practical application than a general systems overview or, worse yet but undoubtedly common, no training at all.

Plus, training for technology shouldn't end with the orientation provided to new personnel. Every employee or volunteer using the organization's technology systems must also have regular opportunities for training, as well as ongoing space for learning and testing tools. Valuable organization-wide training topics include security tests, specific system or software upgrades, and strategy or decision making about the organization's commitments to technology. In addition, position-specific training might include building custom reports and dashboards, managing program-related platforms, or content management and creation.

Also, training for technology shouldn't involve only those who operate it. When technology is a critical element to how an organization operates—or, indeed, is critical to whether an organization can operate at all—it is a leadership component. Every executive director or CEO needs to be part of technology training with the rest of the organization—and needs to reinforce a culture that acknowledges technology as a strategic part of the mission.

What changes in an organization when technology training is understood as leadership development? What shifts in the way training is prioritized when social impact organizations understand themselves to be technology-training centers for staff and community? Technology leadership includes the way technology is budgeted and planned for, and how inclusive processes are facilitated around technology adoption.

Central to technology leadership is the work to align tech to the organization's mission and community needs. In 2020, NTEN published data from Tech Accelerate, a free online technology adoption and effectiveness assessment tool, which showed that over 70% of organizations reported they never or only sometimes educated their employees about how the organization's data and IT systems benefit the organization and its mission.[1] That means that most organizations did not actualize the benefit or strategic alignment of data and technology systems and tools. This is a significant loss.

The benefit to training all employees in the ways the organization's technology tools support the mission and align with the organization's strategic goals is twofold: it supports them in being successful in their jobs, and it enables them to better identify improvements related to their jobs that could have potentially far-reaching positive outcomes. In brief, communicating the broader goals for technology invites all personnel to be part of the ongoing process to improve the ways technology supports the organization.

Center the Community in Your Tech   In addition to technology being integral to every staff member's job, the tools, platforms, and systems an organization uses to collect and store participant data, distribute programs, track service delivery, and communicate all clearly have an impact on the external community as well. As such, including a diversity of internal and external community members in technology planning, prioritization, and decision making is key to successful plans and processes.

Unfortunately, in many social impact organizations, technology projects often receive the least-inclusive planning and processes, sometimes because decisions seem to be set by funders or in grants, or because there are assumptions that only those on the IT team are necessary for participation. Prioritizing the organization's predetermined goals or assumptions about the community's needs in technology planning is not a replacement for or equivalent to directly including community members as participants in technology projects. Social impact organizations can honor the lived experience and expertise of the community in a multitude of ways, and centering the community over funders or other institutions can happen in many situations.

Including community members or program participants in tech projects and committees—whether ongoing or for a finite project or process like strategic planning or redesigning the website—is a valuable way of fostering community–organization engagement. Given their wide range of experience in the programs or services that the organization provides, community members can offer relevant perspective and feedback, suggest new and better options, and highlight challenges that those not participating would not necessarily see or anticipate.

Centering the community also requires organizations to prioritize the needs, objectives, and expectations of current and prospective program participants or service beneficiaries, even when those needs or goals are different from what the organization's strategic plan may have previously said or what a funder has deemed most important. It's not likely that any organization's 2020 planning anticipated a global pandemic, for example. The needs in communities can change rapidly—whether because of something as large as a pandemic or something local like an election or new law. Staying focused on the community's real needs builds trust with the organization or program and that trust equates to power, which the organization needs to use in pushing funders or organizational leaders to realign regularly where the funding or operational goals focus.

Self-determination in a social impact organization's programs and services rightly creates opportunities for participants to set the goals, priorities, or desired outcomes for their participation, whether these be learning objectives or health outcomes or even personal well-being. How do an organization's technology systems enable self-determination? Another way to center the community in technology planning is to implement tools that allow participants to input their own goals, track progress, or provide personal reports on their status or achievements. This might be done during event registration processes, through an individual's profile, or even during in-person service intake appointments.

In addition to the options an organization provides within the technology systems for participants, the selection of software and social media platforms that an organization uses to engage with community members needs to be considered through a careful process with a priority on harm reduction. If the platforms or providers are actively contributing to the issues that social impact organizations are trying to address, investing in those same providers' technologies is in conflict with the organization's mission. Many tools that could fit this description, however, are difficult to avoid as many of these technology giants are nearly ubiquitous in certain fields or business uses. For example, many organizations don't feel they could do the same word-of-mouth marketing and information sharing to those they serve without using Facebook, despite the numerous reports and studies spotlighting cases of Facebook encouraging, allowing, or otherwise incentivizing data misuse, misinformation, harassment, or other material harms for users, especially users of color, LGBTQIA+ users, or those with other identities or needs that make them vulnerable to abuse.

Dee Baskin, the Executive Director of Loan Repayment Assistance Program of Minnesota, has felt this mix of wanting to engage where the community is online along with the worry about what investing in those platforms means. "My nonprofit offers support services to legal aid organizations—helping low-income people access food, housing, disability services, and other basic needs. We have been on Facebook for about ten years. While social media has been a prominent way to engage folks who share our values, Facebook can also act in ways that are antithetical to those values. Even with the benefits, I cannot ignore the fact that there is a company profiting from the vast amounts of data of the marginalized people we are working to help."

There are many factors to consider when making decisions about which technologies and social media platforms to use, and while the decisions will be different for different organizations and communities, it is necessary that social impact organizations make these decisions with the best interests of the community at heart and engage with them about what the decisions are and why. Ultimately, decision making in collaboration with the community will invite better interaction and intentional plans, even if those plans evolve over time as the organization's and community's understanding or needs change.

Build for Inclusion   Honoring the lived experience of community members as valuable expertise also means hiring from the community—which can benefit everyone involved: the organization, those who are hired, and those to whom they provide service. When individuals who have personally experienced the programs or services of the organization deliver those same programs and services to others, their broad perspectives can help them to identify where changes are necessary, especially regarding where participants' needs are unmet.

Note, however, that the benefits of hiring from the community do not replicate the benefit of continued feedback from active participants. NTEN's 2020 Tech Accelerate report highlighted the importance of closely evaluating the way technology supports the organization and community engagement, because roughly 70% of research participants indicated that their organization never or only sometimes reviews how technology affects interactions between staff and clients.

This kind of review is improved when feedback loops and evaluation are frequent and discrete. When feedback is requested often it is usually more comprehensive, and when feedback is requested in relation to specific interactions, events, or programs, that feedback is usually more specific, and thus more constructive. It certainly isn't a new concept to offer a survey to participants after a training event or webinar, but how many of those surveys ask about the accessibility of the program and the technology used, the registration systems, or the personal profile management options that a participant experienced when signing up and joining that event? Asking the right questions is critical to eliciting better feedback—and staff on the team who have experience from the participant perspective likely know the best questions to ask.

Inclusive teams don't happen by accident; inclusive staff teams and technology project teams must be built intentionally. It's therefore important when hiring to prioritize both experience with the organization and lived experience in the community served, especially for the technology teams.

Jason Shim, the Director of Digital Strategy and Transformation at Pathways to Education Canada, has seen firsthand the value of hiring from the community.

> It's one of the best ways to embody the mission and it is a celebration of what we all work towards—when working in an organization that seeks to help students in low-income communities graduate from high school and reach their full potential, hiring graduates from the communities we serve is walking the walk. There's that quotation by William Gibson, "The future is already here, it's just not evenly distributed yet." When it comes to tech teams in nonprofits, I think that hiring folks from the communities you serve is a way to make a dent in the universe by more evenly distributing the future that is increasingly technical—and I'll take it one step farther, it's a way to empower folks with the skills to shape that desired future.
>
> There's a genuine energy and enthusiasm for the mission that is deeply rooted in their experiences. When we've shared as a team our motivations for joining the organization, I hear community members on the tech team articulate that their work is a way to give back.
>
> The perspective and lived experience that is brought to the team also help us build better solutions because the team members already have a deep familiarity with our mission and the community.
>
> For example, we had a community member who is a graduate of our program who joined the tech team as a Product Lead. In this role, he helped to build a platform that offered multiple communication options with students including video conferencing and bulk text messaging.

As a Product Lead, he played a key role in the research and design—when interviewing high school students, it's important to establish rapport and it helped that he was also a graduate of the program who was relatable. For folks on tech teams, it's a thrill when you build something that people find useful; there's an additional joy for community members on tech teams when the community finds a product useful.

The smaller the organization, the smaller the technology team. And so, even with the most intentional hiring, there are only so many positions to hire for—and thus only so many perspectives available. Salesforce's 2nd Edition Nonprofit Trends Report found that 93% of nonprofit respondents reported that a lack of IT or technical staff is a challenge to their organization's adoption of new technologies.[2] Just as members of the community can inject real experience into technology committees, technology managers from outside the organization can be consulted for their expertise.

This approach worked well for Cara Collective, a nonprofit that engages job seekers, employers, and other organizations nationwide to break the cycle of poverty through the power and purpose of employment. Steve Heye, former Manager of Technology for the non-profit, shares: "At Cara Collective we had a team of three people in our IT team, which limited our network, experiences, and expertise. We often relied on bringing in volunteer tech experts as part of a technology advisory committee. These experts offered connections to vendors, new ideas on strategy, ways to cut costs and, occasionally, insight on how to solve the real problem instead of the symptom." Though technology volunteers like this don't necessarily have the context or perspective to take part more deeply in decision-making or planning processes, engaging them in advisory roles is a great option for adding more technical expertise and connections to a team.

Intentionally building teams inside the organization is similar to building a network of peers outside the organization. Regardless of the size of the technology team, hearing and learning from others doing similar work can spark new ideas, lay the groundwork for potential collaborations, and continue to break down traditional silos. Steve Heye credits this kind of sharing and learning as a valuable resource. "Working at a nonprofit with a small IT team is challenging because you may not have peers within your organization who have technical expertise. It can feel isolating, like it's all on you to figure it out, and you are expected to know everything about technology. But technology is so vast that it's impossible to know it all. I have always relied on being in a community with other nonprofit technology staff to learn from each other. Other nonprofits have faced the same challenges as you; connecting to a community of peers allows you to learn from their experiences."

Unfortunately, many technology managers in social impact organizations don't regularly connect with and learn from peers outside their organization. The 2020 Tech Accelerate data showed roughly 75% of organizations report that their technology management staff never or only sometimes shares their experience with other organizations.

Living the values outlined in chapter 2 requires social impact organizations to be intentional about the diversity and inclusion of both staff and project teams. The more intentional organizations can be about identifying where they do not have internal knowledge or experience, and about inviting people in, the richer the feedback and ideas the organization can receive to fuel improvements and outcomes.

Be Intentional in Your Decision Making   Another clear trend revealed from NTEN's years of research is that organizations are more likely to be effective with technology when the staff who manage technology are part of strategic planning. Put simply, the strategic contributions and perspective of technology-responsible staff are invaluable, regardless of their specific job title or position in the organizational chart.

Most organizations address planning every one to five years, creating a strategic plan that mixes visionary direction with more practical annual goals. NTEN has seen that organizations are consistently more effective at actualizing those expectations when these plans include technology, and staff are able to articulate the relationship technology has to the goals and intended outcomes for the community. Salesforce's 2nd Edition Nonprofit Trends Report found that "only 23% [of organizations] have a long-term vision of how to use technology within their organization."[3] Consider the substantial role that technology plays in operations, whether that technology is a volunteer management platform or data management system, impact evaluation dashboard or new program delivery application. If that tech is not included in a strategic plan, all staff who use technology—which is everyone—are left on their own to try to understand the bridge between their systems and the larger direction of the organization. This approach creates confusion, unrealistic expectations, and unrealized long-term goals.

Community members also benefit by seeing technology investments, systems, or data priorities clearly articulated in strategic plans, just as staff do. Sharing the strategic plan on the website or otherwise making it accessible to the community creates an opportunity for accountability, enabling community members to identify where stated goals or outcomes do not meet the community's needs, or that the systems listed are challenging or even harmful to their participation. As new strategic plans are often a number of years apart, the most frequent communication about them may actually be in annual reports or impact statements. These materials shouldn't only focus on program outcomes, but should report on the progress toward technology-related investments and changes so that community members can track when changes may have an impact on the systems they use or even the way they may access their data.

Whether with staff, community members, board members, or other committees, one of the most common ways technology shows up in decision making is by the use of data. Note, however, that though data is a key part of many decision-making processes, not all data sets or sources are applicable or ideal in every situation. So then, what is the appropriate role for data in decision making and evaluation? Regardless of the scope of the data or the decision, the right role for data is where it can illuminate opportunities for further discussion and direct community feedback.

Looking at program evaluation data as an example, many organizations have limited data that is often exclusively transactional, such as which events a participant attended or what benefits they received. Analyzing this kind of transactional data across an organization's programs could surface interesting trends between certain groupings of programs or services. Further, it would be valuable to disaggregate those analyses—by race, gender, age, disability, and even income bracket—to see if there are clear patterns of certain groups receiving different benefits or engaging with the organization in different ways. Note, though, that reviewing transactional data like this is insufficient for strategic decision making. The patterns that emerge from this data are only useful in pointing to areas where greater evaluation is needed, through direct communication and collaboration with community members to bring their experience into context. Subsequent conversations with those members can identify what came of those benefits, whether experiences and outcomes differed among individuals, and what challenges the participants faced in relation to either receiving the benefits or putting them to use. As you can see, none of this valuable detail can be gleaned from simply tracking that certain people received certain benefits.

One point is central to an organization's ability to analyze data and include staff and community members in evaluation and decision making: the data needs to be accessible. In many organizations, only select staff have access to data. Though there are valid reasons for protecting or limiting access to sensitive data about participants and service recipients, there's no reason to limit most staff from having access to nonsensitive data that could help them better serve the mission. And yet, NTEN's 2020 Data Empowerment Report revealed that 75% of responding organizations regularly restricted access to data.[4] Bringing all of the right people and data together allows for decisions to be based on facts, not assumptions.

Intentional decision making calls for purpose-built teams, inclusive engagement with the community, and tactical expansion of information access. Collaboration like this enables planning that builds trust and prioritizes the people served by the mission.

Tech Systems and Investments

We've seen how if an organization's staff doesn't use technology tools consistently, or fully understand their capability, or enter data accurately, it would be difficult for the organization to be effective. We've also seen how the reverse is true: if an organization undergirds its investment in technology with investment in training staff to use it—if it thus emphasizes tech's value by increasing staff technology leadership and by prioritizing best practices in using and maintaining data—then that organization can greatly increase its effectiveness. So, next comes selecting the best technologies for the organization.

Focus on How Money Is Spent   What considerations should technology-responsible staff use for budgeting and planning technology investments? Rather than focusing on the total amount that could be spent, focus on how that money is spent.

Organizations often struggle to make the most of their budget because there is no road map or technology strategy to guide decision making over time. Similarly, many social impact organizations do not regularly evaluate whether the technology they have in place is working—which can perennially frustrate the staff using that tech, and lead to hasty purchasing decisions when it breaks down. The 2020 Tech Accelerate report showed that over 72% of organizations never or only sometimes have a clear process for prioritizing technology needs, selection, and implementation.

Edima Elinegwinga is the Chief Technology Officer at ZERO TO THREE, a nonprofit organization with the mission to ensure that all babies and toddlers have a strong start in life. They provide numerous programs to train and support professionals who support children and their families, as well as policymakers and service providers. Their technology projects include everything from enabling online professional development events for caregivers to data tracking and evaluation to fuel advocacy and policy work.

ZERO TO THREE conducts an annual survey of the entire organization to gather feedback about the way technology is used by different staff and teams, and to identify challenges or needs. Edima notes that these surveys have "really helped give us feedback in areas of opportunities and challenges that we may not have surfaced otherwise." After collecting responses in the survey, Edima and her team analyze the feedback and present it to the organization to review. This intake and reflection process reveals patterns and clear areas of need that affect many people; it also initiates a cycle of aligning priorities and expectations with the entire organization.

Before any spending happens, the whole organization considers where needs are arising and together determines which items they will address in the coming year. Of particular note is the fact that this evaluation process regularly surfaces areas of need that can be remedied through training, rather than more expensive solutions like new tools and products. Edima says, "Before we used this process, people only had assumptions about what was needed and where to spend, because they didn't have data to better understand needs across the organization."

In addition, ZERO TO THREE has found budget savings by annually evaluating where there is overspending on licenses. For example, if a staff person wants access to reports and data but rarely logs in to directly review that data, reports can be set up to be automatically sent to them as often as they like—reducing the need to pay for that staffer's administrative license. Repeat this scenario dozens of times, and the savings can really add up.

When Edima joined ZERO TO THREE, she introduced an agile methodology practice of chunking up technology projects into three-week "sprints." At the start of a project sprint, all related subject matter experts and key stakeholders are tasked with identifying needs, gathering requirements, pinpointing process or user flow expectations, and prioritizing action steps. This group of diverse community members—who hail from both inside and outside the organization—agrees together on the requirements and priorities before the development begins. "Then," Edima explains, "instead of building something for six months or however long a full project may take, every three weeks the group of stakeholders are re-engaged to demo or review what's been built and identify together if things are not aligned with needs or expectations. This really helps ensure we don't have surprises as we build different tools for our work."

Importantly, working in this way enables ZERO TO THREE to make the most of their technology budget because projects regularly pause for review, avoiding overspending or errant development. This saves on both human impact and budget impact, while also building trust and better products. Edima says:

> Sometimes when we demo a project after a 3-week sprint, the feedback is just cosmetic and users don't like how something looks. But sometimes, we completely missed the actual process—even though we all talked about it at the start, once they can see it on the screen they can better describe what is needed or how what was built isn't right. But the good thing is, we've only spent three weeks on this so it is easy to go back and change, then check in again before we move on to the next phase. This has been received so well because the entire organization knows what the IT department is focusing on and can see that every department has time and projects included throughout the year.[5]

Evaluation and interaction create a process for investing in technology that brings needs to the fore and generates regular opportunities for cost savings and intentional budgeting.

Focus on Accessibility   There are many ways that accessibility is considered—or not considered—in organizations. From physical entrances to internet service to language interpretation to digital functionality, accessibility is a very big topic that requires care, attention, and commitment. As with many areas of technology use and investment, focusing on accessibility from the start avoids having to spend time, energy, money, and heartache redoing decisions, designs, and workflows.

According to Pew Research Center data from a US survey in 2021, "62% of adults with a disability say they own a desktop or laptop computer, compared with 81% of those without a disability." In addition, the report states, "Americans with disabilities are three times as likely as those without a disability to say they never go online (15% vs. 5%)."[6] Unless organizations take time to be intentional about engaging with community members with disabilities, the probability that those members are learning about the organization's programs and services on its website is much lower than for other groups. Remember that what works best for one group does not always work for another— but thoughtful and strategic technology planning and implementation can enable users to access an organization's information and programs.

The Web Content Accessibility Guidelines, or WCAG, provides a global standard for online accessibility;[7] unfortunately, many organizations don't ensure that their websites or other digital tools, events, and programs meet those standards. WebAIM[8] and other similar tools help identify which portions of a website are not accessible by the WCAG standards. For many organizations, accessibility improvements are needed in areas that can be easily addressed, such as adding alt text for images and ensuring that styling structures are used consistently so that screen readers can parse the text. Even if the organization doesn't have technical control of a system or tool—say, for example, a program team relies on a third-party tool like Google Hangout or Zoom for virtual events—accessibility issues can be addressed within those tools, including options for how folks can dial in by phone or computer, and additional services for translation and captioning.

Of course, staff accessibility is important too. Diverse applications exist for addressing how staff are trained, supported, and able to use technology. Of primary concern in this realm is the fact that organizational policies that expect staff to provide their own computers—often called Bring Your Own Device (BYOD) policies—disadvantage staff based on income, personal experience and knowledge, and more. BYOD policies are neither equitable nor accessible. Employees have different levels of expertise with which to select and maintain tech products, as well as different financial resources with which to buy them. Organizations need to provide all the technology tools—hardware and software—that are required for success at the organization, as well as the training and accommodations or assistive technologies and supports to enable staff to use technology in their work.

Note that accessibility to websites, technology tools, and even programs or services is not a discrete investment "just" for people with a specified disability. "Disability" is a wide-ranging term, and many accommodations or customizations to tools and programs help community members both with and without various disabilities. Cognitive differences, chronic health issues, and even the realities of changing schedules and caretaking all affect how a community member or staff person may need to, say, call into a meeting instead of joining on video—or follow a transcript of an event, or require live support, or prefer asynchronous communication.

Equity concerns everyone. And disabilities, personal needs, and health challenges can all change over time—so just because someone didn't need an accommodation previously doesn't invalidate the request today. The more effectively an organization addresses accessibility issues of all kinds—and thus removes barriers—the more effective it will be in fulfilling its mission.

Make Data Systems Equitable   Data is a subject of many contradictions in many social impact organizations. Sometimes organizations collect valuable data, like community feedback or qualitative evaluation, but then neglect to incorporate it into decision making. Sometimes organizations neglect to collect data in areas that could better surface equity issues, or improve how the organization communicates with and serves the community. For example, NTEN's Data Empowerment Report found that over 60% of respondent organizations never collect the pronouns its participants prefer, and just over 20% collect pronouns only occasionally. Without collecting pronouns, the organization can't communicate with individuals without making assumptions about their identity.

Jude Shimer, the CRM Manager at Center for Popular Democracy, experienced this particular neglect in multiple ways in interactions they had with organizations they engaged with as a community member. As they explain, the way organizations structure their data systems internally has external impacts that create barriers and distrust for program participants and supporters.

> Common practices in nonprofit fundraising impact trans and nonbinary community members. I've experienced this as a donor, but fortunately have also had the opportunity to help organizations break those habits.
>
> I once tried to submit an organization's donation form, but the form required a salutation, and there was no gender-neutral option such as Mx. I contacted the org to see if they could make the field optional and/or add Mx, but they apologetically told me their technology didn't allow them to do either. So I didn't donate. The experience left me suspicious of the organization—if they couldn't accommodate trans or nonbinary donors, how could I be assured they accommodated trans and nonbinary people in the communities they served? And the issue is self-perpetuating: pushing away trans community members removes their voices and hampers organizational growth.

If a community member does make it through an intake process—whether donating or signing up or participating in an event—what the organization does with their data matters. As Jude shares, it is important that organizations ensure there are systems to honor and protect the accuracy of data directly provided by users.

Data sharing can negatively impact trans community members. I once became a member of an organization without entering any gender data, but later received a membership card for "Ms. Jude Shimer." Updating contact information with data obtained somewhere else may add an outdated salutation or gender to that individual's record. By referencing bad data, an org can misgender a community member, and misgendering is often an extremely unpleasant experience that will impact a person's impression of the org.

Worse, I had to call the organization twice before I stopped receiving emails addressed to "Ms. Jude Shimer." Each time I was assured my salutation had been removed. Organizations often lack a protocol for making sure that updates to a person's name, pronouns, salutation, or gender are preserved. If a community member contacts an org to correct their information and these corrections are later undone by, for example, a rushed data update, misgendering that individual could cause them to lose trust in the organization and feel that the org's inclusion efforts are hollow.

Recently, I joined a cohort of trans tech professionals and allies from several nonprofits to provide feedback on the inclusivity of a specific company's tools. The company not only was receptive but later proactively sought our feedback on additional features. Whenever a company's technology does or should store data on individuals' identities, the company ought to routinely engage communities of that identity in their planning and design processes.

There is a lot to balance with data in social impact organizations: not being extractive by collecting more data than is necessary, while also collecting enough data to understand the communities and the organization's impact. It is critical for intentional service delivery and program evaluation that organizations collect data including race, disability, gender, and age; but there are many instances and communities for which that data or information—about, say, immigration status, service history, or even relationship status—in the wrong hands could have dangerous outcomes. If data could cause harm if shared, it's critical that both the collection processes and the storage tools are secure. For example, collecting sensitive data on a clipboard at an event is not safe, but collecting that data on a secured and protected laptop or tablet for data would be both safe and efficient, as the information would be added directly to the database. Security is key for all systems where data is stored, yet, according to the 2019 Global NGO Technology Report, only 41% of social impact organizations globally use encryption technology to protect their data.[9] The data that community members trustingly share with social impact organizations still belongs to that member—so, it is essential that that data is stored securely.

Honoring self-determination with data in social impact organizations means ensuring that community members have the flexibility to identify in authentic ways and not be restricted to demographic options that don't match their identity. For many social impact organizations, collecting data from community members is at least partly in compliance with reporting expectations from funders, including government and philanthropic grants. But just because a funder uses outdated, inaccurate, or otherwise different data structures for their own evaluation and reporting, that does not mean the grantee social impact organization needs to push those same structures onto community members. It is important that data management and use policies explain how an organization stores and secures constituent data, as well as how they will use it—including how they will adapt data to reporting requirements.

Furthermore, centering the community in data use means that organizations should use caution with tools for predictive analytics, and evaluate the presumptions those tools use both in their algorithms and comparative datasets. If an organization is working with communities already experiencing historic and systemic harm, it is likely that a predictive analytics tool negatively reinforces stereotypes or assumptions that may not be accurate. Relying on those tools, then, sets the organization up to perpetuate harm or to maintain systems that disadvantage or prevent community members from receiving the full breadth of their potential supports.

It is an honor to be trusted with the caretaking and safekeeping of data from community members. It behooves social impact organizations to prioritize safety, accuracy, and self-determination so as to best position themselves for success.

Invest in Tech for Today and Tomorrow   The COVID-19 pandemic disrupted everything across the globe. And while no multiyear strategic plan could have predicted it specifically, the sudden need to change how and where staff do their work is not an unreasonable inclusion in a technology road map. Important opportunities open up when organizations don't just look at the way technology supports the mission today but also look at how the investments made today could further effectiveness or flexibility in the future.

In NTEN's 2021 Tech-Enabled Operations Report, respondents were asked how well-prepared their organization was, either technologically or culturally, to shift to remote work because of the pandemic. Nearly one-quarter (23%) of respondents reported not being prepared technologically for staff to work from home.[10] This is a disappointing outcome—given that remote-access and cloud-based tools are not new, and given that folks with disabilities, caretakers, staff with children, and other groups have for years requested options to work more flexibly.

While of course an organization can't anticipate every manner of emergency, disaster, or community change, it is possible to infuse expenditures for immediate needs with an investment in the future.

At ZERO TO THREE, a learning management system (LMS) was implemented to support some of the professional development programs they run throughout the year. This online system integrated data and processes so that community members could smoothly register and participate in events, and the organization could easily track and manage participant lists, participation history, and more. Given the nature of the training events, some program staff and the community groups they worked with were used to working offline. But when the pandemic hit, making their more localized, offline processes less feasible, they were swiftly set up with online program delivery through the LMS used by other areas of the organization. How did this come about? Edima and her team already knew that the LMS could support many more programs than just the original groups involved in the implementation, so the LMS did not include tightly fitted customizations exclusive to a single program area. This broader application view meant that when the time was right—or, in this case, was forced upon them— the process of onboarding new teams and programs to the platform was fairly straightforward.

"Technology planning is key to successful implementation today," says Edima. If an organization has a broad view of both its current needs and potential changes down the road, that organization doesn't necessarily need an IT road map or multiyear development timeline specifying decisions years in advance. Instead, organizations can develop documents or dashboards that indicate when current tools are up for renewal, when programs are expected to expand or change, and where staff have the highest areas of need. Focusing on those details would enable staffers to make decisions and investments today that can ripple forward to support effectiveness over the long term.

Develop New Models for Change-Making

Many social impact organizations and efforts have been encouraged to believe they are in competition for resources and recognition. As such, it can feel imperative to constantly do something "innovative," announcing an original new approach. But this scarcity mindset erroneously pits organizations against each other—even, at times, against the communities for whom they are working in service. Shifting out of this scarcity mindset opens up the space for collaboration, learning, and values alignment.

Build Power with Shared Infrastructure   A direct counteraction to the mindset of competition is to share the very tools an organization relies on with others to reuse and further build on. This could work in a number of ways. For example, some working in the climate action sector have shared a single back-end database that houses comprehensive knowledge about the campaigns and topics that interest various constituents; as a result, they've been able to distribute more integrated calls to action.

Mala Kumar, Director of Tech for Social Good at GitHub, sees every day how open source software is developed in support of a social need, or the way an organization's work in one area can be redeployed all around the world by others. She shares:

> One widely cited and successful example of open source software is DHIS2, which is led by the University of Oslo. It's now been deployed in 70+ countries around the world at some level—some instances are at the national level like in Kenya; most of them are at the sub-national level like a district or region. It's really important because, as we consider the different systems—like electronic medical records for individuals, on up to the health management system to see where resources may be or what are the national rates of a certain disease—DHIS2 is on that aggregate level. This information is really important when

it comes to public health funding, for example, because we could see an uptick in COVID-19 or HIV, and DHIS2 plays a critical role in enabling that work. They started this as an open source platform and, while there are people in national and regional teams managing the software for their use, developers have also built apps that run on top of it that add customizations for localization needs.[11]

When more of the tools organizations use are shared, funding and development work can be devoted to improvements to those tools or customizations for different use cases—or even additional pieces of software that enable different programs stemming from similar technical needs. Sharing infrastructure also accelerates learning, because groups can report how they have succeeded, and where others have encountered challenges putting the same technology in place. These collective lessons result in a better product for everyone—not to mention the goodwill and camaraderie that stem from such trusting collaboration.

Budget for Learning and Testing   Learning is one of the most valuable aspects of technology processes and projects for social impact, but it is not always free. When planning and budgeting for technology, organizations should consider how and where there may be space to invest in staff time, processes, or budget to enable active and regular learning and testing. As Edima explained in relation to their three-week sprints, some of the opportunities for testing and learning may come from processes that ensure there are frequent opportunities to pause development and get feedback from project teams and stakeholders, quickly identifying issues or changes before more development takes place.

Central to focusing on learning is remembering that technology is going to change. GitHub's Mala Kumar refers to technology as "a living document" that we should expect to be constantly updated. This means that any information an organization learns about community needs—say, through program evaluation or feedback—can and should be applied to the technology that supports those community members and programs. This evolution of technology is a gift and a benefit, not a burden.

QUESTIONS FOR WHAT'S NEXT

Social impact organizations are an important part of the fabric of resources in our collective work to create an equitable world, but technology can greatly influence their effectiveness. Creating a culture of technology leadership across an organization is just as important as embedding community-centered models in every technology project. Reclaiming Leftover Cuisine's case study showcased the opportunities we have for intentional technology development to accelerate impact, and lessons from various practitioners showed the value of staff training, building inclusive practices, and developing shared infrastructure.

Technology will continue to change. Social impact organizations need to continue investing in technology training for all staff, improving accessibility, and strengthening the opportunities for community voices and priorities to be central in the plans for the organization's work and systems. The following questions are designed to support social impact organization staff in having valuable conversations about the values and community-centered processes outlined in this chapter with technologists, funders, policymakers, and community members.

Social Impact Organizations

Questions for those working in and with social impact efforts to ask their peers:

- What tech tools are working well for you to manage projects? For managing constituents? What tools didn't live up to the hype?
- Do you use a change-management process when rolling out a new technology internally?
- What needs are you still trying to address for your staff?

- How do you ensure your staff knows how to use and continually uses technology?
- Where do you seek information on what tech is useful for social impact organizations and how to adopt that tech into your organization?

Technologists

Questions for those building technology for social impact to ask those in social impact organizations:

- What does "technology" mean to your organization? Who on your staff is comfortable discussing how to use tech to improve their operations?
- Do you have documented processes for how you work with staff and with clients? If not, are you open to creating this documentation?
- Who are the champions for technology in the organization? Who are the champions in each team?
- How are community members involved in decision making within the organization? How can we increase community-member input into technology projects?
- How is technology addressed in your strategic plan? How do these plans meet that strategic goal?

Funders

Questions for those in positions to fund social impact and technology to ask those in social impact organizations:

- What is the next internal process you want to either (a) develop and apply technology to, or (b) improve the technology for?
- What percentage of your staff participates in either gathering requirements or defining user stories? What percentage of your staff participates in testing?

- Do you have the internal capacity to deploy tech? Or do you need to be connected to (or provided with?) a service that deploys tech for social impact organizations?
- In what ways are you engaging community members so as to ensure these technologies relevantly address their priorities?
- What have you learned from previous iterations or attempts similar to this one that can be brought into this next attempt?

Policymakers

Questions for those creating and enforcing policies around technology and social impact to ask those in social impact organizations:

- How are you working in coalition to surface priorities?
- What examples or proof of concept do you have from your community/work that makes clear working in coalition is a priority?
- What data do you have that supports harm reduction in policies for your community?
- Can you help us understand why this hasn't gone through or been successful in the past?
- What other policies do you feel are successful that we could scale or learn from?

Communities

Questions for community members to ask those in social impact organizations:

- How will your systems, data policies, and practices honor our expectations for consent, opt-ins, and safe and secure data?
- How do you support us advocating for ourselves? How can we continue to own our stories and experience with you?
- How is our lived experience centered in decision making?
- What structures are available to formalize our leadership in the organization?
- How do we contribute to setting the organization's goals?

Chapter Four

Changing Technology Development Inside and for Social Impact

Technological development truly changes how people live and interact with the world. With advancements over the past decade, people can imagine sending themselves into space, learn to dance from nimble robots, and order whatever they want via the latest phone app. As the creators of these programs and devices, technologists "determine what can be improved in their industry and how to incorporate new technology, find new ways to resolve problems, and further develop various processes."[1] Given this high standard and supposedly universal expertise, many people expect technologists to quickly enter the social impact space and create inventions that "single-handedly" feed the hungry around the world, solve climate change, and improve access to and outcomes from education—and then spontaneously dream up the next invention.

This, of course, is not how things work. The social impact sector tackles challenges based on systemic inequity and injustice, problems that can't be solved with a simple invention. There must be a recognition that the big technological solution is in fact a combination of many small solutions. Also, the expertise technologists bring can help create a new and better world, but only if the technology is appropriately designed in the context of local communities and with deep understanding of the multifaceted elements in play, such as the root causes of the problems, interventions that can make progress possible, and the network needed to realize sustained change. This understanding must derive from how these problems are actually experienced, not from how they are interpreted from the outside. There must be a recognition that the big technological solution is sometimes a combination of many small solutions. Furthermore, technologists in future social impact organizations must strike the balance between (a) building basic technology systems, such as simple databases to store information on clients, for the social impact sector, and (b) identifying ways in which new, never-before-used technology can be created and applied to social challenges. These complex challenges present a high bar for technologists to meet, beyond "just" deploying complex tech. They must understand the power and potential of technology, as well as its limits and constraints; they must also be able to determine when technical proposals are documented pipe dreams and not possible within the constraints of reality, as well as when not to pursue a technical solution at all.

As we outlined in chapter 1, when people reference "technology" in relation to social impact organizations, they mean everything from Information Technology to organizational management tools to advanced techniques for improving operations; in other words, technological tools that help every department within an organization as well as program delivery and interaction outside the organization. Staff can quickly become overwhelmed by the countless technology questions they must ask themselves:

- Do we have enough computers and cell phones?
- Can people securely log in remotely?
- Do we have servers in our offices or cloud storage space?

- Do we have software to track and contact our donors?
- Do we have software to track the care we provide to our clients?
- Do people have a seamless experience when they visit our website?
- Have we used data science to analyze the effectiveness of our training systems?
- Do staff have the tools they need to be effective in their work?

Historically, many organizations in the social impact sector have treated the answers to technology questions as something for the tech department (or person) to decide in a vacuum—because, as has been argued, they know technology best and it is too complicated for the average person to make an informed decision. The reality, as we discussed in chapter 3, is that to support a functioning society, technology must extend—not replace—the social impact organization's missions. The technologists who join the social impact space, similarly, must join with the mindset of learning and supporting the organization's mission—rather than simply inventing what seems like the easiest and most obvious fix.

Technologists in the social impact sector will serve a broad variety of functions. Therefore, we consider a technologist to be the technical designer, developer, or implementer of any solution that helps advance an organization's mission. For the purposes of this chapter, "technologist" can represent either a single individual or a technology company developing tools to address social impact issues. And as we progress to creating the connected world we envision, we have different questions to ask:

- How do we build new tools to support this world?
- How do we ensure that multiple perspectives influence and develop tech in equitable ways?
- How can we better share information and tools across communities?
- How can we sustain and evolve solutions so that they change as the people relying on them change?

In chapter 3, we examined how social impact leaders must plan, budget, and integrate technology as a component of all programs and services. In this chapter, we will examine the ways technologists intentionally extend the mission and impact of social impact organizations: by expanding access to themselves, by continually checking for consistency between code and values, and by consciously deciding when to exercise technological caution versus when to push organizations into something new.

CASE STUDY: JOHN JAY COLLEGE

Dara Byrne is the Associate Provost of Undergraduate Retention and Dean of Undergraduate Studies at John Jay College of Criminal Justice, a public senior college of the City University of New York. In 2016, Dara wanted to know how she could better support the college's students up until they graduated. The overwhelming majority of support services were geared toward freshman studies—but still, after doing the majority of the work required, some students didn't complete their senior year. Dara wondered what more the college could do to help more students graduate.

Around the same time, DataKind—a nonprofit whose mission is to harness the power of data science and artificial intelligence in service of humanity—approached John Jay College. DataKind had received funding to work in the education space, and wanted to know if John Jay College was interested in partnering. What made the outreach unique and interesting, Dara reflects, was that DataKind proposed to discuss and collaboratively define a problem to solve—whereas most tech companies approached with some version of "We know what your problem is, and we know how to solve it for you."

Working together, the John Jay College staff and DataKind staff defined two questions to answer: (1) Could they identify students in need of support who were likely to drop out?; and (2) What were some of the factors that could influence a student's decision to leave school before finishing their degree? Reflecting on this process, Dara comments on the validation she received at the time. "The DataKind team made me feel heard. They showed me what it is to be believed with the expertise you have." The DataKind team identified and reviewed the college's data, then led discussions with the college team about both their understanding of the data and the limitations of the data from a technical perspective. The DataKind team also spent time in the college's systems to ensure that what was to be built would be able to run within the existing environment without requiring the purchase of a lot of new equipment.

The collective team decided to focus on students who had completed 75% of the credits needed to graduate—or 90 points out of the required 120 points. The team tested more than 20 different modeling approaches, algorithms, and combinations of models. In the end, the team created two sets of models using machine learning, each designed to predict the likelihood that a student will graduate within four semesters after completing a minimum of 90 credits of coursework.[2] The tool generates risk scores for students and provides insights into the factors that may lead to students dropping out. In the words of Michael Dowd, the lead DataKind data scientist on the project: "The final tool takes in data (such as grades, length of time at the school, test scores, credits taken per semester, etc.) and predicts the probability of whether or not students will graduate within a specified amount of time. The tool also shares with the user information about which variables contributed to the overall probability and why."[3]

Dara conceived the Completion for Upper Division Students Program (CUSP), as "a college completion program designed to prevent drop out among undergraduate students in their final semesters and instead help propel these students across the graduation finish line." Through CUSP, Dara's team uses the tool created with DataKind "to then provide tailored interventions to students based on these risk levels, including general text message reminders, personalized advising on how to meet remaining academic requirements, strategies and completion grants for overcoming financial barriers, and post-graduation planning and referral resources."[4]

Laura Ginns, John Jay College's Vice President for Public Affairs and Strategic Initiatives shares:

> Before implementing CUSP in Fall 2018, we projected that, without any intervention, only 54% of our seniors at or above the 90-credit mark would graduate by the end of two years. In the two years following the Fall 2018 implementation of the CUSP program, however, 85% of students who were at or above the 90-credit mark that term have graduated within two years. Thanks to CUSP, this means that over the two years, 900 more students than projected earned their Bachelor's degrees. CUSP has been central to John Jay's increased 4- and 6-year graduation rates, which rose 8 percentage points and 4 percentage points, respectively, in just two years.

These stats alone are impressive, but Dara says the impact within John Jay College is even more widespread. "You don't expect confidence, capacity building, and culture change to come out of a technology collaboration, but that's what happened," Dara remarked. Throughout the development process, the DataKind team explained to the college staff what data was being used and how. As a result, today the college staff who interact with the developed tool—whether the director of institutional research or the frontline staff working directly with students—can explain what information the tool uses and how it assesses the data. In addition, the success of the study resulted in new partnerships being formed within the college, as multiple departments became interested in using the tool or providing information to it. Dara's team, now confident in their ability to understand how the technology works, expects more from tech companies approaching them with their flashy, proprietary tools. She comments: "Now that we have had these experiences with DataKind, when tech companies won't explain what's in the formula, it raises a lot of suspicion."

The DataKind team was able to document the lessons learned—and the code developed—from the partnership. This information has been shared with similar organizations to help them understand how they too could benefit.

Ultimately, the experience gave Dara a new confidence and strengthened her credibility within the institution: "For those of us who are BIPOC leaders, being listened to with a sense of curiosity is a big difference. It's unusual to encounter, especially in the land of technology. But now, I know what to ask for."

DEVELOPING TECHNOLOGY FOR SOCIAL IMPACT ORGANIZATIONS

The DataKind and John Jay College partnership shows that good things can happen when technologists are intentional about learning from their social impact partners, thorough in considering various technical approaches, and deliberate about selecting and implementing the ideal model. It also illustrates how detailed understanding of the technology being deployed—in this case, predictive modeling—is necessary to responsibly execute a technology solution. In addition, it underscores the importance of technologists explaining the technology and the implications of technical decisions to their customers in plain language. But one of the more significant truths the DataKind and John Jay College partnership demonstrates is the power technologists have to shape outcomes.

The responsibility of distributing power lies in the hands of the technologists. This is because technology can automate or define so many ways that social impact organizations operate. The time and frequency of system updates can dictate when and how social impact employees work. An organization's ability to provide computers and phones to employees (rather than requiring them to supply their own devices) equalizes who can perform their work. The weights given to particular variables in algorithms determines who receives services and who doesn't. Furthermore, in a world where policies and regulations often don't affect the most current technology, or how the social impact sector can use technology, people who design technology become de facto policymakers, with the ability to turn on and off who gets access to services based on a few additional lines of code.

These implications are serious, and technologists must take their role with a respectable amount of gravitas. And, in turn, it is important for us to acknowledge and respect the responsibility that technologists have in creating a more equitable world, and to ensure they are empowered to steward this responsibility well. To follow are our guidelines for doing so.

Develop a Thorough Understanding of Both the Capabilities and Limitations of Technology

The social impact sector is not a place for technologists to experiment for the sake of experimenting, or to practice their skills until they're "ready for the private sector." Technology work within communities is its own discipline, because the work greatly impacts people's lives and livelihoods. And so, technologists in this field need to be experts in their craft, regardless of whether that expertise is gained via formal educational settings, boot camps, apprenticeships, on-the-job-training, or otherwise. Whether on the IT side, the software development side, or the user design side, technologists must understand the ins and outs of the technology they develop, deploy, and manage. Of particular concern is understanding the downstream effects of technology systems—and, accordingly, when a technology should not be deployed if it wouldn't ultimately further the necessary goals.

Historically, the temptation has been to assume that tech is always inherently helpful. Surely, the assumption goes, adding tech services will help an organization increase its impact or improve efficiency. For example, as the COVID-19 pandemic raged in 2020, Google and Apple developed and deployed contact-tracing apps to help track and manage infections. Yet, in the summer of 2021, when the United States saw some of the highest COVID-19 case numbers at that point, only 2% of cases were being tracked in these apps.[5] This is one of many instances where technologists failed to understand the social context of the situation, and pushed for a technical solution that ultimately failed to maintain interest. (In fact, the authors of this book are considering writing a book titled "I Can Fix Your Social Impact Problem with an App, and Other Fairy Tales.")

The social impact sector requires technologists to constantly learn about the cultural and societal environments in which their technology is deployed. It also requires an "accessibility first" default design suitable to all potential users to include rather than exclude. In many ways, newer technologists might want to practice their skills in the private sector until they're ready for the social impact sector.

Develop a Thorough Understanding of the Situation Being Addressed

No one expert in technology, regardless of that person's lived experience, will also be an expert in (all) social impact areas, with knowledge of the root causes of the problems, interventions that can make progress possible, and the network needed to realize sustained change. For this reason, technologists must approach their work in the social sector with humility, acknowledging—to themselves and others—that they don't know everything, and asking questions so they can learn from fellow members.

One starting point is to develop an understanding of the social impact ecosystems beyond simply the technology. Humans have evolved to live in community with each other—to such an extent that many socially isolated people suffer from depression and anxiety.[6] Accordingly, a technologist's ability to support relationships—with nontechnologists, with the people using and affected by the technology, and with the organizations that serve the community—is crucial for success. Michael Dowd, the DataKind data scientist who led the development of the tool from the preceding John Jay College case study, describes it this way. "It was very important to explain to John Jay College what we were doing because of their deep subject matter expertise with the school's data. Their insights led to changes in how we developed the models that supported the tool; in fact, the decision to build two separate models, one for students who had started at John Jay College and one for students who had transferred into the College, came from conversations between DataKind and John Jay College."[7]

The DataKind team partnering with John Jay College got it right: they listened to the people most closely affected by the challenge, and they developed a solution together. This approach ensures representation at decision-making tables—effectively redistributing power to those most affected by the decision. The technologists first brainstorm a solution alongside the social impact practitioners. They then develop the technology, test it in its intended environment with those who will be using it, and modify the technology as needed.

Within this process it is essential that technologists push for technically sound applications, but also know when to not use particular technology. Let's say the challenge is a policy one; it won't matter how efficient a system you've built to match people with housing options if the local government hasn't allocated enough affordable housing. Or perhaps the technology can't be used without discriminating against populations, such as an Artificial Intelligence tool designed to help recruiters filter through résumés but the tool actually filters out women.[8] A variety of other reasons can be summed up as determining that using technology in a particular manner will not only not advance the cause, but it will likely inflict harm on someone directly or indirectly touched by the technology.

Negative impacts that disproportionately affect people of color have been documented again and again—not just in the private sector, such as regarding access to housing, attacks on social media, and more, but also in the social impact sector. Although many argue these unintended consequences are unavoidable, this is not the case—and their effects can be lessened by, first, an expansion of racial literacy. As defined by Daniels, Nkonde, and Mir, racial literacy "is a new method for addressing the racially disparate impacts of technology. It is a skill that can be developed, a capacity that can be expanded." Sasha Constanza-Chock demonstrates in their book, *Design Justice*, that "when design processes do not consider inequality in design . . . [they] are structured in ways that make it impossible to see, engage with, account for, or attempt to remedy the unequal distribution of benefits and burdens that they reproduce."

Inequality in design doesn't just affect people of different races. A number of other communities are often overlooked in technology design. Even though disabled people use technologies every day, accessibility is often an afterthought for technologists. Only 2% of websites are accessible, meaning for the 1.2 billion disabled people in the world, performing a *simple* search online is not all that simple.[9] accessFind, which claims to be the world's first search engine for accessible sites, provides users only with accessible sites. The creation of this program highlights the need for accessibility to be designed from the start, so that everyone has the option of accessing the tech.

We must also take note of intersectionality in these conversations. People aren't only Indigenous or only female, for example; they can be an Indigenous female, and therefore subject to compounded effects of inequality in design.

Expand the Idea of Who Technologists Can Be

The three main guidelines we've discussed are essential to the goal of ensuring equity in tech. But as for empowering communities, the greatest impact can come from expanding who we see as able to be a technologist and who has access to technologists throughout the development process." According to 2014 data from the Equal Employment Opportunity Commission, in 2014, nearly 70% of the people employed in the US tech sector were white, whereas whites made up about 60% of the US population as a whole.[10] Six years later, the diversity reports published by major tech companies such as Alphabet, Facebook, Google, and Twitter, revealed that their stats had remained mostly the same.[11] We must expand the diversity of people who become technologists, with their lived experience, personal expertise, and varying perspectives. It is important that technologists, and the organizations they serve, be held accountable to and be in relationship with those affected by their products. Also note that technologists should intentionally bring more people into their process and into their work, even if these additional individuals are not developing code; there are many other roles with critical perspectives in projects of this sort.

The organization Code the Dream is living this dream. It "recognizes that people from immigrant backgrounds and communities of color have great ideas and will play a huge part in our 21st century economy." And so it provides coding courses to students who are predominately from immigrant, historically underserved, or poor communities.[12] As cofounder Daisy Magnus-Aryitey reflects, "There are so many people from underserved backgrounds who want training and experience, and there's a lot of work in the public interest to be done." A team of senior developers at Code the Dream constantly works on public interest projects; their team of senior developers regularly takes on apprentices, usually individuals who have completed Code the Dream's beginning and advanced courses. These collaborations have led to many interesting tech projects that, for example, connect individuals to North Carolina government agencies that help them take advantage of debt relief programs and restore their driver's licenses—thereby also restoring the ability to work and stay connected.

Another particular solution—developed in part by the children of farmworkers—that provides farmworker-support organizations better tools for understanding the actual needs of farmworkers. The programs,

Conectate and Vamos, are accessible via a website or an app. Given that the initial developers had such a strong sense of the farmworkers' lived experience, they were able to build applicable focus groups that included both farmworkers and existing organizations that served farmworkers, which yielded invaluable information. The collaboration also facilitated introductions to and relationships with organizations who adopted the software. As a result, organizations can be alerted when farmworkers are moving into their service area, and can proactively prepare to distribute food, clothing, and other services. To build on this sort of benefit, we need to ensure that a diverse range of individuals are brought into the decision-making and design processes. This is the power that comes from expanding who can be a technologist and allowing individuals to build technical expertise while respecting and engaging their identities and communities.

Respect Communities by Using Data Responsibly

Ultimately, the development and deployment of tech systems is a way to empower individuals and empower communities. When done responsibly, this empowerment can also support organizations' abilities to serve their clients and minimize harms inflicted on systemically and historically marginalized populations. One practical concern is the use of data. As the prevalence of data in the social impact sector continues to grow, so do calls for data-driven decision making and data collection; however, especially because this sector collects personally identifiable information, as well as data that reveals intimate details of their clients' lives, organizations and therefore technologists have an imperative to collect, store, and use data responsibly.

This effort starts with minimizing the data collected in the first place: only what's needed for the project, and nothing more. Although it can be tempting, of course, to collect additional information for a theoretical future positive application or a potential customization, that temptation needs to be quashed. Next, organizations must consider who needs access to the data collected—and then regularly revisit these assumptions. It is essential to restrict access to the data because doing so decreases the chances of data leaks outside the organization. Finally, technologists must think critically about what data is shared and how. Is information presented in ways that nontechnical employees can easily understand and interpret it? Is data shared in ways consistent with what was communicated to the information provider—usually an individual—at the time the data was collected? Following these and other user-centered data and privacy practices enables technical systems to properly safeguard the personal information they possess.

BUILDING NEW MODELS FOR TECH DEVELOPMENT

The progress we want to see doesn't stop with changes to the design process. All technology must be built and then maintained. After a tool has been deployed, it will need to be periodically checked to make sure it still works: that underlying data hasn't changed, that access lists haven't been altered, and that supporting technologies are still relevant. If that maintenance can only be done by a select few individuals from outside a community, the solution will not empower the community. And so technologists must later move past designing *with* affected communities and strive to transfer ownership *to* those communities.

But before we can transfer ownership, we first need to develop the tech to later hand over. To follow are some guidelines for doing that.

Buy, Borrow, or Build?

After relationships have been built and inclusive decision-making processes have been formed, the technologists ultimately have to build and deploy the technical solution. When doing so within a social impact organization—whether assessing a new program to run in the cloud computing environment or building a new website—one of the first decisions technologists must make, in coordination with organizational leadership, is whether to develop a unique solution from scratch or to buy one off the shelf.

Developing a new, completely custom solution allows technologists to design something that will tailor to the organization's and to the community's needs. It allows flexibility, provided there is enough time and funding available, for the technologist to include all of the desired features into the solution. If an organization imagines a new process and a new way of teaching people or serving people, a technologist can create software that enables them to do just that. In contrast, purchasing or adapting existing technology often allows for a quicker path to adoption for the social impact organization. Speed, however, often comes at a cost in flexibility of business operations; the organization often has to at least slightly alter its processes to fit the workflows and structures of the not adapted technology. Maybe an organization used a two-step process to check people in for services, for example. If the software they purchase requires three steps, the organization will have to update their process so that it can be handled by the technology.

To help determine which development to use, technologists should ask themselves:

- Does the social impact organization have a limited percentage of staff who would be comfortable using and maintaining the technology?
- Are the staff pressed for time? Will waiting for a custom solution have a negative impact on the organization's ability to provide services?
- Will the technology be designed "for all" and not undergo explicit checks against implicit bias?
- Will a third party have access to or own any data used by the technology? If so, will a third party be able to share or publish the data?
- Will a third party be able to prevent the organization's access to the technology without consulting with the social impact organization?

If the answer to many of these questions is no, an off-the-shelf solution might be ideal. But if the answer to a majority of the questions is yes, then it's likely the technologists should seek out products that were specifically designed for that social impact sector. If none can be found, then a custom-made solution might be the way to go. As for the questions themselves, it is crucial that social impact organizations retain the ability to control both the access to data and who can turn on and off the solution. Decisions such as these allow for equitable treatment of people and safeguarding of information and operations.

Once a decision has been made about whether to purchase existing solutions, modify existing solutions, or develop new solutions, technologists must consider what type of development and provider to pursue. If the decision is to acquire existing technology, options could be chosen from a traditional private sector company, the open source community, or the nonprofit tech development community. To follow are guidelines and some caveats on all these.

Private Sector Technology   Private sector companies often enter the social impact sector with the intention of adding a "for good" component to their broader portfolio. They often assume that tools that work in the private sector can readily transfer to the social impact sector, generating many of the efficiency and productivity gains that the private sector has enjoyed. However, products designed to succeed in a marketplace that values shareholder return over all else may not be appropriate for the social impact sector. In some cases, such as with digital storage space, the functionality needed in the social impact sector and in the private sector are similar enough that the technologies can be easily applied to the social impact sector. In other cases, such as with customer relationship management software, the technology may need modifications before being applied in the social impact sector. And in other cases, the technology should not be used in the social impact sector at all.

Research led by Joy Buolamwini and the Algorithmic Justice League, highlighted in the documentary *Coded Bias*, is an example of this idealized transition not working in practice. In the film, Buolamwini discusses the research with which she revealed that facial-recognition systems are significantly less accurate for people with darker skin—especially women with darker skin. Although the overall accuracy percentage of such systems was deemed sufficient by private sector institutions—such as law enforcement and landlords—clearly this technology is inaccurate with traditionally marginalized populations. And because these populations deserve equal rights and equal treatment, the technology that we apply to the social impact sector must work for everyone. And so, if technologists pursue private sector products to be used in the social impact sector, they must always question for whom the technology works and who is failed or excluded by the technology. Once those important details have been ascertained, the next step is to learn whether the project's social impact leaders consider the trade-off acceptable to the community.

Open Source Software Can Strengthen the Ecosystem   Open source software is code that is designed to be publicly accessible—anyone can see, modify, and distribute the code as they deem fit.[13] Flexibility and transparency are two of the biggest benefits for using open source software. Because the source code is freely available, technologists have the option of implementing the program as written or modifying the code for their specific needs via a fairly straightforward method. In addition, many open source software programs are regularly used and maintained by a community, so bugs can be reported and fixed, and technologists can learn from each other. These same communities are often vigilant about stopping any nefarious behavior, so the software generally stays secure. Open source software is often, but not always, free. And, you somewhat get what you pay for; even with developer communities, there is no guarantee of a quick resolution to any issues one may find.

Mala Kumar, the Director of GitHub's Tech for Social Good Program on the Social Impact Team, has seen a number of open source projects used for social impact. She shares how one particular open source software program already developed for a social impact organization was able to be quickly modified and applied to another situation. "One example that Clayton Sims, the CTO of Dimagi, told me was how important CommCare became in COVID-19 contact tracing. A few big tech companies made an attempt at building a contact tracing app, but quickly realized how complicated it was and stopped. Meanwhile, CommCare had been developed in response to Ebola, and could be quickly and appropriately repurposed. Suddenly, CommCare was being deployed in San Francisco, not just in Central Africa. Saving that kind of time and money in emergencies is critical."

Community Tech and Nonprofit Tech Must Work for Social Impact Workers, Too Community tech and nonprofit tech represent development communities that explicitly design for the social impact sector in ways that prioritize equity and justice. The online Community Technology Field Guide states: "Community technology is a principled approach to technology that is grounded in the struggle for a more just digital ecosystem, placing value on equity, participation, common ownership, and sustainability."[14] The technology solutions produced by these communities tend to be designed for everyone—including those on the margins of society—in ways that prioritize care of data, access, and ownership. If the products are relevant for another organization's project, social impact technologists can bring these products into their environments with a considerable amount of trust.

Although the social impact sector has many organizations working on similar challenges across the globe, the incentives aren't always aligned for organizations to easily collaborate on implementing technology toward their mission. Also, organizations are often funded for their individual work without being allocated time or resources to share the lessons learned across the sector. But if we can figure out ways to collaborate on technology, and have technologists drive some of the knowledge sharing, we'd greatly enable the social impact programs. Technical learning communities and technical consortia can help with this. NetHope, which brings together large social impact organizations for this purpose, and NTEN, which provides resources and a community gathering space for technologist practitioners, are among the many organizations creating the space for the intentional sharing of the dos and don'ts of technology in the social impact sector.

Most of the discussion in this chapter has been focused on technology's ability to extend the social impact organization's mission in serving people. We need to remember, however, that the needs of the organization's employees are important too. The tech we develop needs to work well for employees. As an example, let's say an organization builds a website that allows its clients to easily access benefits. The clients are well served, but on the back end employees must be physically in an office during set hours, combining digital information submitted via the website with physical papers and charts. How organizations do their work is as important as what they deliver to the communities they serve. As technologists work on projects in the social impact sector, it is essential that the roles of organizations' employees are explicitly included in and enabled by the technology being designed. This calls for ensuring those employees are supplied with hardware and software, and that embedded accessibility features (such as closed captioning) guarantee equal access. As an added bonus, such efforts would advance the employees' work experience and skill sets.

Ethics, Security, and Privacy Must Be the Foundation of Technology Development

In recent years, conversations about "ethics in technology" have entered mainstream technology conferences and mainstream media. Scholars in interdisciplinary studies, such as the field of science, technology, and society, for example, have been studying these issues for decades. Many women of color have investigated why and how unchecked technology systems are detrimental to the function of society. For example, Dr. Safiya Noble, MacArthur Fellow and cofounder of the University of California at Los Angeles Center for Critical Internet Inquiry, has challenged "the harms algorithmic architectures cause and shows the necessity of addressing the civil and human rights that are violated through their technologies." In her book *Encoding Race, Encoding Class: Indian IT Workers in Berlin*, University of Washington professor Dr. Sareeta Amrute examined the interplay between conceptions of race and programmers. There are many, many others. The Founding Director of the University of Michigan's Digital Studies Institute, Dr. Lisa Nakamura, gave TED Salon talk on "The Internet Is a Trash Fire and Here's How to Fix It," which reflects just some of her research.[15] There are many, many others.

Still, some of the current, mainstream conversations about ethics in tech seek a quick fix. The authors of this book have attended technical conferences where someone poses the question, "What one thing do I need to do to have ethics in technology?" or "Can you please share a list of ethical algorithms for me to use," or "How do I do a quick check before I take my product to market to make sure it doesn't cause any problems?" If only it were so easy.

Kathy Pham, Co-Director of Mozilla's Responsible Computer Science Program and member of the World Economic Forum's Advisory Committee on Tech Ethics, approaches integrating ethics throughout technology development this way:[16]

> When I think about technology and ethics, I think about three things: Who are the people impacted whether or not they use the service; what fields and disciplines do we deeply involve in the decision making and product development process (history, philosophy, law, policy, race and gender studies, humanistic studies, art, and more); and which parts of the product, engineering, and design cycles we can leverage or intervene to drive change. What this might look like:
>
> • If a team is debating using machine learning on a group of images to determine safety, is there someone around to share the Broken Windows theory or the concept of safety for whom?

- In the early stages of development as teams design their user interface and what fields to put in a form, does someone default to how gender has been a Boolean (yes or no) value in the past, or that zip code should always be required despite the complex issues that arise with zip codes?
- When designing a product or service that is intended for everyone, in the case of government for example, are the most vulnerable populations considered first, or is the product designed to an ideal set of circumstances like ability to access the internet, read words on a page, see colors, understand the flow of the site to be able to get through the whole page?

Ethics in tech requires ongoing, intentional reviews of the work being done. The process of innovation is iterative, and as a result, there will be negative externalities to be mitigated in each iteration. Ethics in tech, then, requires truly inclusive processes as described in this chapter. It necessitates technologists intentionally questioning potential sources of bias in the data used to drive programming and decision making. It requires considering the assumptions or historical issues embedded in the system. (For example, if you are trying to develop a tool that identifies what it takes to be a leader, and your test data is from companies that historically have hired only men, then your tool will conclude that to be a leader, you should be male.) And it requires being willing to *not* implement the solution if testing reveals that the technology excludes or harms people.

The choice to not implement a developed technological solution is tough to make, especially when considering the many demands on time and financial resources in the social impact sector. However, the cost of implementing unethical tech is much greater. In early 2021, DataKind moved to wrap up and transfer a data science program to a partner organization they had been working with for months. In the final reviews prior to deploying the program, DataKind realized there was a problem: the partner organization that had collected and shared the data could not confirm that consent had been provided for all the data collected. Because ownership and protection of data is so important, DataKind ultimately decided to not deploy the program. Even projects by social impact technologists in close partnership with social impact organizations, with good intentions from all involved, are not immune to the challenges of developing ethical technology; this is why checks for bias, discrimination, and ethics must be performed from the very start to the very end of the development process.

In addition to building in ethics throughout the design, development, and deployment lifecycle, technologists must also consider protections—specifically, privacy and security—from the very start of the design process. Social impact organizations hold a treasure trove of deeply personal information that readily targets nefarious actors: that is, hackers and hacktivists. With pressures to move quickly in the social impact sector, there can be a temptation to skip over privacy and security details at the start—with the intention of adding them at the end of the process, when there's more time or greater knowledge. Unfortunately, this good intention is frequently left unfulfilled.

The Citizen Clinic "support[s] the capacity of politically targeted organizations to defend themselves against online threats"; their Cybersecurity Education Center offers many examples of how social impact organizations should think about and approach security. The Citizen Clinic has helped voting rights organizations develop a more secure account system to control who has access to what shared email and software accounts. It also helped an abortion fund defend itself from threats of data breeches, counterfeit fundraising pages, and online harassment by moving digital assets to more secure digital spaces, defining access controls, and updating systems that "had previously been too difficult to safely and efficiently use."[17] This last consideration applies to all technology development in the social impact space: it must be appropriate for the environment in which it will deployed—neither overly complicated just for the sake of using fancy technology, nor so unsophisticated that it leaves organizations vulnerable.

Imagine a Bright Future

We know that the technology of today isn't everything we need for everyone who needs it. We also acknowledge the technology skepticism referenced in chapter 1, which derives from the many documented ways that technology can do harm. That said, as technologists work in the social impact sector, they should not be constrained by the failures of yesterday and simply fix what is currently broken. They should boldly create what's needed for the communities they serve.

Technologists can also intentionally build community by sharing with social impact leaders the specific challenges they are working to address. A 2021 report on Building Career Pathways for Diverse Public Interest Technology Entrepreneurs highlights organizations that were effective because entrepreneurs, drawing "from their own lived experiences stemming from their identities, . . . identified a gap that was felt closely and sought to close it." The examples include a child of a Chinese immigrant who created a "nonpartisan platform that enables people to select the issues they care about and then receive alerts before Congress is about to vote on any of those issues." In another, a founder who has several family members with diabetes used "tech to bring people together to make it easier to navigate the healthcare system for Black and Brown folks."[18]

When interests such as these combine, technologists truly can advance a social impact organization's mission. Indeed, many private sector companies, such as banks and online retail stores, have become tech companies without calling themselves tech companies. Some academic institutions and government agencies also have large tech departments that drive their operations. A great deal of opportunity exists within the social sector to integrate technology into the core operations of organizations.

Technology within social impact organizations isn't just IT; it's a more comprehensive approach that touches staffing, programming, delivery of services, and evaluation. Organizations must use technology to make decisions, improve mission operations, and more. Appropriately designed technology means responsibly using advanced technology in the right situations. By applying the complexity and limits of technology, including a diverse group of people throughout the design and development process, and consistently checking for ethical decision making enshrined in code, social impact technologists can play a critical role in sustaining a transformed organization. There is a difference between simple technology and simply explained technology, and social impact technologists should be willing to provide both. The ability to translate between technical complexity and social mission is key to creating an equitable power structure in which impactful work can be done. The tech that comes next is completely up to us. Let's ensure tech teams and tech companies are inclusive and embedded in the social impact sector, working hand in hand with the communities they serve.

Of course, technologists and social impact leaders are only two pieces of the puzzle. Their visions and collaborations must be funded in ways that empower them to center equity and justice in the work they do.

QUESTIONS FOR WHAT'S NEXT

Technologists working in the social impact sector have the opportunity and responsibility to help social impact organizations expand their missions through the thoughtful application of technology. When technologists make intentional decisions about when to use and when not to use particular technologies, bring along community members while applying ethical, security, and privacy frameworks, the technology can empower social impact organizations, just as the DataKind & John Jay College partnership empowered college administration.

Engaging with technologists to generate inclusive, responsible, community-centered tools can be challenging if you don't know where to begin and the language is unfamiliar to you. The questions below can be used to guide conversations with technologists to start collaborations that can build the tech that comes next.

Social Impact Organizations

Questions for those working in and with social impact efforts to ask technologists:

- How have you learned about our particular work and affected communities? How will our communities be included in the design and testing processes?
- What happens if your technology fails? Who will be harmed?
- How will you ensure that I understand how the systems are being used? How the data is being used?
- How will you ensure that your technology will work with the technology and systems we have today? How will you ensure that the cost to maintain your technology won't be prohibitive for us?
- How will you ensure that your work advances at a reasonable pace, that it respects the organization's time, and that it's ultimately delivered on time?

Technologists

Questions for those building technology for social impact to ask of their peers:

- Did you partner with organizations and individuals throughout design, development, and testing?
- How did you determine that this solution you propose is the right approach? What did you decide not to do and why?

- What lessons do you have to share on building capacity and leadership in the community that will be maintaining the technology?
- What specific tools and techniques were applicable in this situation and why? Do you have code to share?
- Are there solutions that you developed here that could be used elsewhere? What organizations or individuals can we talk to, to make that happens?

Funders

Questions for those in positions to fund social impact and technology to ask technologists:

- What are the expected long-term maintenance needs for the technology?
- How will you teach the organization staff how to interact with and maintain what you develop?
- What support will the organization need to make successful maintenance happen?
- Based on what you learn in the design process, how will you communicate if changes are needed?
- How are you connected to the communities impacted by this project? How will they be involved?

Policymakers

Questions for those creating and enforcing policies around technology and social impact to ask technologists:

- How have you ensured that people will be able to access your technical solution?
- How have you mitigated bias in your technical solution's development and implementation?
- Where does the tech solution end and the need for new policies begin? In other words, what are the limits of the technical solution?

- Where are the components of the technology that are not currently protected or directed by policy?
- How does this technology maintain protections for the user's ability to control their data?

Communities

Questions for those creating and enforcing policies around technology and social impact to ask technologists:

- How can our lived experience be prioritized in the design and development of the tech?
- How will you invest in our training and knowledge so that we can be part of ownership in the long term?
- How will you ensure I understand how the systems and data are being used? How will you ensure I control the way my data is being used?
- How will you ensure our consent will be requested (now and in the future) in relation to the ways data is used to make decisions for and about us?
- What's the plan for making sure we can continue to use this technology after you're not involved?

Chapter Five
Changing Technology and Social Impact Funding

With the onset of the COVID-19 pandemic in March of 2020, many offices cleared out as usual on a Friday—but then no one returned the next Monday. Almost overnight, millions of people across sectors and industries transitioned to working virtually and remotely—a work style that had long been resisted by many managers. This nearly spontaneous phenomenon was enabled by technology. But for many social impact organizations, especially those working at a local scale and through close community interaction, moving to a virtual model simply wasn't possible in one night or one week, because the technology tools and the organization's skills and strategies with them weren't positioned effectively for staff to pick up working from wherever they may be.

During the early weeks of the pandemic, NTEN hosted free, public, online office hours for staff in social impact organizations as well as consultants, technology providers, and funders to ask questions and share tips as many organizations were struggling with their new work realities. The questions received ranged widely—from a nonprofit employee in Alaska wondering if it was "allowed" for staff to work on their personal smartphones, to an organization in Washington, DC, looking to migrate their full office to the cloud, to a global organization seeking example equipment stipend policies. These conversations led to funders inquiring about their own staff's most pressing needs, as well as technology providers highlighting their solutions that were potentially applicable to needs across the sector.

But, ultimately, quandaries on how to adopt and adapt technology to meet community needs, how to operate securely and accessibly from wherever, and how to construct policies and strategies for using technology equitably were not unique to the reality of 2020. These challenges and questions and efforts are as old as digital technology itself.

Of course, the community challenges and the prevalence of technology didn't start with the COVID-19 pandemic. Many social impact organizations had always relied on ill-suited tech; the pandemic merely forced some long-delayed, long-necessary decision making. Similarly, opportunities for funders—philanthropists, individual donors, investors, and even at times nonprofit organizations—to accelerate social good also preceded the pandemic. The problem is that many funders value the visibility of funding new things and partnering with prominent technology companies, which leads to funding for projects that build technology outside the community. But if financial resources were prioritized and invested in those deploying and affected by technology so that they could build what they need, then everything from research and development, piloting, adopting, and scaling technology could move more effectively.

Chantal Forster, the Executive Director of Technology Association of Grantmakers, has observed this dynamic within the philanthropic sector:[1]

Historically, grantmakers have implicitly asked social impact organizations to minimize operations in order to maximize outcomes but few have asked what are the long-term impacts of this strategy. For those funders willing to underwrite technology, they're often focused on headline-making tools related to a specific program rather than the nuts and bolts systems required for an organization's very viability. These "boring basic" systems such as CRM, cybersecurity, accounting systems, and more are often outdated and neglected. What grantmaker is willing to fund a network intrusion detection system, an overall security strategy, and staff training on cybersecurity awareness? The result of this neglect is an increasing dependency on philanthropy to scrape together the dollars needed for modern and secure operating infrastructure, IT strategy, and skill-building.

We can accelerate impact by changing how and who we fund as well as by developing technology for social impact. This calls for rethinking and reworking the models, expectations, and values that organize our systems of investment, from grantmaking to seed funding. Foundations and corporate philanthropy efforts, venture capitalists, and individual donors can all play a role in shifting what funding means and can do in the service of the social good.

In chapter 3, we addressed the importance of social impact organizations and leaders being intentional and comprehensive in planning, budgeting, and integrating technology as a component of all programs and services. In chapter 4, we discussed the need for technologists to value partnerships and context. For those efforts to be successful, we also need to change how technology in and for social impact is funded.

CASE STUDY: OKTA FOR GOOD

Funders hold an inordinate amount of power in social impact contexts as the deciders, influencers, and resource holders for so much of what social impact organizations can do. Technology companies, which provide products as well as funding and resourcing for the sector, have even greater influence given the number of ways organizations may be looking to them for support. Okta for Good, the social impact initiative from Okta, the leading independent identity provider, offers an educational lesson in how to remain humble amid that power and how to center the community in decision making, planning, and building programs.

Okta for Good was first formed out of the company's 1% pledge, announced in October 2016, which included Okta's original product donation offering for nonprofits. Pledge 1% is a movement in corporate philanthropy to encourage companies to pledge 1% of their employees' time, 1% of their product, and 1% of their equity and/or profits toward giving back to nonprofits and communities.[2] Erin Baudo Felter, the Vice President of Social Impact & Sustainability at Okta, reflects, "When I started at Okta in 2017, there were maybe two thousand companies who had taken the pledge; today there are over ten thousand."

More pivotal to Okta for Good than the pledge was the process through which Okta's founders and leadership envisioned long-term strategic philanthropy: by setting aside 300,000 shares of Okta for the Okta for Good Fund. In early 2017, Okta planned for an Initial Public Offering (IPO), wherein they would offer up shares for public investors and transition from a privately held company to a publicly traded company. One of the many documents any company files in the lead-up to an IPO is an S-1 filing, essentially a disclosure of basic business and financial information that potential investors considering buying stock review to get more details about the company and its intentions. Okta's S-1 outlined the Okta for Good Fund, the dedication of 300,000 shares to fund it, and the priority that this portion of investment had for the company. As Erin explains:

> For Okta's founders, it was important to them that they sent a signal to any investor that was considering buying Okta that said, "If you invest in Okta, you will also be investing in Okta for Good." This was an important and intentional moment to

make it clear to employees, customers and investors that these were the values of the company they wanted to build.

The job in front of Erin when she started in early 2017 was to take the 1% pledge focus areas of time, product, and dollars to build initial programs. She remembers sitting down with the founders to discuss the mission and focus for Okta for Good: "It could have been anything, it was a blank slate. I presented all kinds of options and ideas and I'll never forget the response because it was so clear. Our CEO said, 'If we're not helping nonprofits do better with technology first, then we should just go home. That's who we are and that's what we know.' It was very simple and it gave me permission to start the journey of helping nonprofits with technology and infrastructure, which has led to everything we do now."

That pragmatic and authentic vision of the CEO opened the door for Okta for Good's philanthropic focus to bend to the community's needs. "It wasn't about putting the company's name in headlines anywhere, or grandiose expectations that we alone would solve anything," says Erin. "Instead, a focus on who they are and what they do—quite frankly the best way to do this work anyway."

In 2017 and even today, giving product as a primary definition of charitable investment is common. But, as Erin explains, it can't be the only way companies give:

> A focus purely on getting more nonprofits to use your tech without an equal investment in enablement and education can lead to what we don't want, which is companies patting themselves on the back for giving away millions of dollars of software that doesn't actually get utilized. The reason that companies don't invest equal measure in enabling the use of its products versus donating licenses is that it is so much more expensive to enable it. It requires people's time, people that have to help with implementation or deliver training. It isn't scalable for a free piece of cloud software.

In addition to Okta for Good's production donation option, they have also implemented a pro bono professional services program to receive free technical project help, as well as a donation program for their trainings so that nonprofits could access, at steep discounts, the same training programs big clients pay for. In addition, the Okta for Good Fund allowed them to dig into what philanthropy could mean for their efforts as well. Erin explains the process for learning that Okta for Good took on:

> We started to orient our philanthropy around supporting the better use of technology across the nonprofit sector. We started very small with one grantee, and then two, and then three. What we were trying to do in the early days was to give where we could learn. So we looked for organizations that we could fund, but also partner with and learn from—better understanding their communities and what pain points around technology existed. It helped us start small, learn, and do the work quietly instead of calling ourselves experts or providing support where it might not be most needed.
>
> Years later, we continue to be really close with those early partners—organizations like Nethope, NTEN and FastForward. It led to what would become our Nonprofit Technology Initiative and our $10 Million, 3-year commitment launched in March 2020. It was the culmination of all we had learned so far: that no one wants to fund technology capacity building; no one is talking enough about it; and that the topic of technology is often inaccessible to funders and nonprofit boards and leadership teams. Add onto that, many tech companies approach nonprofits with their products. Even if it is a donation, there is the assumption that the organizations know how to use the tools. This is often not the case; there are big systemic barriers.

Deeply learning—with and from initial grantee partners and the organizations and communities they serve—helped Okta for Good dig into those barriers.

The team identified the need to directly address the overhead myth and nonprofit starvation cycle funding problem—which can't be solved with tech donations or pro bono services, but can be solved by talking to funders and raising awareness about the impacts and ways to change. It became clear that this could be a role for Okta: talking louder and talking to groups it could influence, such as other funders and technology companies. Erin shared: "We want organizations to fund nonprofits the way that provides the most value, which is multi-year unrestricted giving as a default, in part because we know that's how any capacity is funded but particularly because that's what is needed for funding technology capacity." Because Okta's funds are limited—$10M over three years is generous but the company knows it won't solve everything—they have taken the approach of funding ecosystems and networks where they can provide one-to-many impact. And Okta is supporting the advocacy piece of systems change with a fellowship program, lifting up the voices of the nonprofit technology leaders doing the work who need space to network, speak, and write.

Okta for Good's prioritization of listening and learning with partners and communities has led to strong relationships forming across the philanthropic, technology, and social impact sectors. As Erin notes, "I think because we've listened and focused on forming relationships, we are now becoming the de facto experts in our sector. What's going on with nonprofit tech? Talk to Okta. Part of that is because if you listen and learn, you earn that opportunity."

Despite doing many things right, including committing to supporting social impact organizations, engaging as learners and partners to better understand the needs, and investing real resources in the sector, Okta for Good isn't perfect. What's important is that they know and admit that as well. Realistically, there is no single "perfect" approach; the goal is to continue learning, growing intentionally alongside the community, and reimagining over and over what more is possible.

INSIDE THE PRACTICE OF CHANGE

Put simply, funding technology for social impact work is tantamount to funding social impact work. Social impact work today cannot happen in a sustained, shared, or scaled manner without technology supporting either operations or delivery, or both. For example, an organization maintaining their donor list and program participant data exclusively with paper forms or a local Excel file will be unable to fully analyze participation or efficiently distribute communications and donation appeals. Or, an organization expecting staff's personal cell phones to be adequate for customer service and program delivery will be missing the opportunity to use more effective, sophisticated, and operationally appropriate models for engaging groups and the chance to create opportunities for people to join in the ways that are most accessible for them.

There's no path to funding technology in social impact organizations and efforts without that investment supporting the outcomes and impact for the community. All too often, funding for social impact work does not include the technology necessary to do that work well, which is the equivalent of paying a contractor to build your home but not the lumber to build it with.

Furthermore, funding technology in social impact work needs to cover more than just technology tools and systems. An efficient, effective operation requires the selection, customization, implementation, and maintenance of software, hardware, and other applications. And so, technology funding must include the resources to adequately train staff, support necessary upgrades and maintenance, and engage community members in research, design, implementation, and evaluation.

Many think that nonprofits can sufficiently benefit from the technology built for sales or other for-profit industries that is offered "free of charge" to social impact organizations. The trouble is that, for some, such software is similar enough to what is needed that it looks worth using, but they find it can only be made to work after painstaking customization. And neither is it actually free. Even if products are "free" to download or install, the necessary staff training, customization, hosting, maintenance, integrations, and more will all need to be paid for in ongoing ways.

If we value those who benefit from social impact efforts, we need to learn how to fund the technology that will get us closer to a better world.

Funding Tech Deployed for Social Impact

Social impact organizations deliver some of the most crucial social services in our communities. They advocate for the protections and investments necessary for our schools, environment, and arts to thrive. They supplement gaps in care for seniors, children, and others in need of assistance. In 2019, 12.3 million people worked in nonprofit organizations in the United States.[3] The International Day of NGOs by the European Union estimates that the number of people employed in a nongovernmental organization will exceed 100 million globally by 2030.[4]

Yes, there's a lot of important work being done. And there are also a huge number of people trying to do more of that work right now. Shifts in funding approaches could result in immediate improved outcomes, increased scale of impact, and transformed organizational effectiveness. How do we get there?

Fund for Comprehensive Technology Needs   There's a common saying that "technology is free like kittens are free." Imagine your neighbor's cat just had an unexpected litter, and you excitedly bring one home. Then the spending starts. Kittens need food, and containers in which to serve it and store it. They need a litter box and litter. They need perches to climb up to and toys to play with. Then there are the visits to the vet, and the carrier to get them there, and the medications prescribed there. After a couple years, you look around your house at the furniture and curtains shredded by claws and realize that that kitten was free for just about five minutes.

Technology is a real expense because it is the foundation of a social impact organization's ability to operate. As noted earlier, funding should include all the costs associated with making and keeping technology working for the mission, as well as the space and resources for staff to continue building skills for using and managing changing technology.

"So, how much do you need?" This question morphs in conversation to, "How much is the right amount?" But no set amount is relevant and appropriate across a single mission area, let alone around the world.

Plus, this isn't about simply spending more (and more). Since 2005, NTEN has conducted annual research in the nonprofit sector about the ways organizations budgeted for and managed technology investments. The conclusions consistently showed that technology used well could facilitate organizational effectiveness at any budget and staff size. The organizations that were most effective with technology invested and spent intentionally; how money is spent is more important than how much is spent.

That being said, it is clear that there is a range where organizations of many sizes are all able to do well. Effective technology budgets for social impact organizations are at least 3–5% of an organization's operating budget. At it happens, this range is lower than the average technology budget in for-profit companies. But note that comparing for-profit and nonprofit spending is like comparing apples to oranges, especially given the vastly different ways in which organizations budget and define budget areas, as well as the difference in applying technology spending toward sales versus toward program support.

Aki Shibuya, an operations leader at a Seattle-based foundation, reflects:[5]

> The funding sector has had conversations about needing to dispel the overhead myth for years, but there are still a number of foundations that perpetuate it by granting only a small portion of total funds to help an organization with its daily operational expenses or by placing an extremely restrictive measure on funds that could otherwise be leveraged in more effective ways. . . . In order for a social impact organization to do its best work, it not only needs the technology and the space to do so, but also the people that bring their knowledge, expertise, and dedication to the work. Without investing in the staff and resources—the categories that are often seen as "overhead"—the programs that serve the community will not be as strong as they can be. Ultimately, if funders, donors, and other philanthropic-minded individuals are there to support social impact organizations because they want to actually see societal change, they need to support these organizations in the way the organizations need them to show up (and get out of the way to let them do the work).

It is also critical to remember that a technology budget is not something that only surfaces at times of system redesigns, implementing or integrating new tools, or otherwise launching technology. The technology budget is needed year-round for the maintained and continued upgrades and improvements that come with sustaining technology infrastructure.

Don't Conflate Product Donations with Funding   We mentioned above how technology companies often include in their "for nonprofits" or charity programs the donation of their products to social impact organizations. Those product donations can be undeniably helpful—in an organization that already has the right infrastructure and staff training. But if the free or discounted products have a term limit, the benefit can turn costly, and the "charity" model reveals itself as the sales pipeline it actually is. It is not capacity building, and it is not a donation.

In actuality, providing free products that have real costs for the corresponding implementation, maintenance, and training is an inequitable and unethical revenue pipeline. This is because organizations most in need of low-cost or free product options become dependent on the offering provider because they likely don't have training or product adoption budgets and staff in-house. The technology provider should understand what kind of investment is necessary for success for any type of client, and that information needs to be clearly articulated as part of the product information, especially when marketed for free to social impact organizations.

Plus, we can't underemphasize the importance of a product's design being crafted for its precise purpose. Otherwise, the product is often unusable unless money is spent on customization and adjustments. Mismatched products can also have a negative impact on an organization's data, community, or programs; for example, when a participant logs into their profile and notices they are called a "customer" or a donor's preference for giving by check isn't acknowledged in emails asking them to "donate now" on the website. These are everyday examples of how systems can break down trust and confidence between community members and the organization simply because of the technology tools in place.

Yet another downside is the fact that when products not designed for social impact work are marketed to such organizations, it contributes to the myth that social impact organizations aren't legitimate organizations worthy of best-in-class technology built for them, and instead should be grateful to have access to tools other industries consider excellent. This ignores the reality, of course, that social impact organizations are certainly deserving of purpose-built tools and that many of the products for-profit companies consider key to their work are successful for them specifically because they are such a perfect fit for the use case, one that social impact organizations don't necessarily share.

But that's another apples-and-oranges assessment. Social impact organizations are some of the most innovative, creative, and solution-focused entities there are, especially given the immense needs they meet under incredible constraints. The truth is that such entities heartily deserve investment. The technology that fuels their work becomes part of their impact, and thus becomes part of the wider solution of doing good.

Limiting your "investment" in the social impact sector to your free product licenses is inequitably accessible to organizations that already have the most resources, staffing, and technical expertise. As such, the charitable aims of product donation programs benefit organizations who are already more privileged with technical or other resource supports.

Aki Shibuya explains:

> While funders should not dictate solutions (including products or methodology) or consultants, they can provide support beyond the grant itself. . . . Where restricted funding can be helpful is to designate capacity-building dollars for organizations so staff can take the time to learn and develop skills on whatever topics and/or products are relevant for them. Funders also could leverage their relationships with other funders and grantees to connect organizations to new thought partners and networks. Most importantly, strong relationships of any kind require listening and communication. If grantees express needs or challenges that arise, funders can and should look to see how they can help them. This could look like lifting restrictions on any previous grant because priorities have shifted, or tapping their network to surface appropriate resources that match emerging needs.

If funders want to give away tools, apps, or products—for free or reduced rates—they should make sure they are also giving away cash grants to organizations, whether or not they use the funders' products or not. Fund social impact work and organizations' success with technology by actually funding them with money. Unlike many foundations that maintain rigid application processes and reporting requirements, technology providers can offer access to financial support without those hassles.

Support Product Choice　Consider the following scenario. A foundation that wants to see the impact of their grantmaking identifies a database or other data management tool that meets its own needs and preferences. The foundation negotiates with the vendor to purchase a certain number of licenses (or to cover the implementation for a certain number of grantees) to have the product set up with customizations determined by the foundation. Then the offer is promoted to the funder's grantees as a new opportunity to receive support from the foundation.

This is the idea of group purchasing taken in the wrong direction, even if it is offered with the best of intentions. This is because this model doesn't leave room for appropriate strategic alignment by the organization with their staff and community members. Nor does it honor the fact that individual organizations and their communities must be part of the process of deciding which technology tools and priorities best align with their needs and mission.

Because few social impact organizations feel financially secure enough to not engage with private or corporate philanthropy, many organizations feel an obligation to try to participate when a funder expresses interest, even if that interest means an offer to provide preselected technology solutions. The number of organizations that apply or respond when funders put out these offers is not in itself a sign they are valuable. Quite frankly, philanthropy has fueled a scarcity culture in the sector, through actions like these in two ways. First, scarcity is reinforced by positioning the foundation, which has more resources, staffing, and access to technical expertise (whether in-house or paid for), as the only one making the technology decisions—implying that the less-resourced, smaller organizations are not qualified to do so. Secondly, scarcity is reinforced by the competitive nature of private philanthropy today, where any opportunity to be in closer relationship with a funder is sought out and is likely pivotal to determining whether an organization receives other opportunities and funding in the future.

Not only is this model an extension of the issues related to product donations where the full cost of success isn't accounted for or supported, but also funders dictating the use of specific products inappropriately, even inadvertently, promote certain tools as a requirement for access to other funding opportunities. The power that funders already hold in relationship to social impact organizations is highly imbalanced. Promoting specific tools to grantees exacerbates this power dynamic with very real negative outcomes for the organizations, who must then try to put tools into use that weren't selected by their teams and community, are likely not an adequate fit for their needs, and without plans for maintaining and sustaining the technology over time.

Always Fund Technology Capacity   If a program, project, building, event, service, or initiative is worth funding, it should be worth funding successfully—and technology is essential to that success. As such, within every funding portfolio, grants must include funds to cover the technology needed for the application's focus.

Make it clear to social impact organizations seeking funding that technology is an expected and accepted part of every grant application budget. Specify this view in funding information, including in grant application forms or budget templates, and in discussions of necessary technology investments for project or program success.

Ensure that program officers have the training to discuss technology capacity and needs. This does not mean that every program officer and funder needs to be a technologist or hold a specific certification. It does mean that program officers should be comfortable and confident discussing technology-related challenges, needs, and plans with grantees, both those needed for the success of the organization and to any specific program or project. As we discussed in chapter 3, to be successful, it is essential that social impact organizations support every staff person in gaining and growing the skills necessary to make technology decisions and put those tools to work toward the mission. The same applies to funders investing in those missions.

Program officers or investment managers don't have to work alone on this, especially in funding organizations that have their own skilled technology teams. Chantal Forster, Executive Director of Technology Association of Grantmakers, believes funders are missing a valuable opportunity to connect these two internal teams:

> There are few opportunities for foundation IT and program staff to communicate and coordinate technology-related grantmaking. While foundation operations staff such as IT leaders are fully aware of the basic technology needs for any modern organization, they typically lack access to program dollars. Conversely, program staff with access to grantmaking dollars aren't necessarily knowledgeable about or interested in nonprofits' technology operations, preferring to focus on program-related tools or breakthrough innovations. And even when there are potential opportunities to support technology operations, it's rare that program staff consult their IT colleagues for advice or proposal review. The result: nonprofits don't get the funds they need for that "boring" stuff like digital tools, skills training and enhanced cybersecurity. Bright spots exist in the form of IT leaders such as David Krumlauf with the Pierce Family Foundation or Leon Wilson with The Cleveland Foundation, both of whom shape technology support programs for grantees or fund a portfolio of tech-related grants.

Consider dedicating portfolios or program areas specifically toward technical capacity. This would enable organizations to seek funding for projects that include selecting and migrating to new systems, updating current user processes for more integrated or accessible engagement, or redesigning online sites and program delivery platforms. These investments will produce benefits across the organization's programs and teams, but many of these efforts come with a number of unknowns that make it impossible to budget the up-front costs into other program grants. If you dedicate funding for such technological undertakings, you communicate both that it is appropriate for organizations to take on such investments and that funding is available at the level necessary for a full project's success.

Fund technology projects on long-term timelines. It takes time for a social impact organization to adequately analyze needs, engage their community, select and customize the necessary tools, and implement them in equitable ways to provide input and adjustments iteratively as community members and staff learn and test the tools directly. Ideally, reporting on grants like these can be minimal (as is ideal, in fact, across all grants) and focused on surfacing lessons that can support broader learning by the funder, the community, and the sector. As we discussed in chapters 3 and 4, technology development is essentially testing and learning (or failing) over and over, so a grant that supports technology projects should not consider changes or revisions to be anything other than the iterative learning that is necessary for success.

In the tech sector, it's completely expected that tech companies and start-ups will receive funding for pre-development work: landscape and market analysis, interviews and focus groups with anticipated user groups, and even initial prototyping for viability testing. This pre-development work helps to ensure a successful build-out and implementation; it also helps to clarify priorities once full development begins. So then why can't we do the same with social impact organizations? Many funders already invest in the equivalent of this pre-development work in other areas, such as feasibility studies, land use plans, and even legal groundwork for new initiatives.

As noted earlier, funding technology in social impact organizations means funding more than products; adding decision making, implementation, maintenance, and training to the total would ensure that funding is comprehensive to the real work for social impact organizations to use and maintain technology effectively.

Align All Assets with Mission   While grantmaking is not the only option for financially resourcing social impact efforts, it is of course an important one. And yet even grantmaking is not meeting current needs.

Increased grant support could yield exponential benefit. Rather than increasing or maintaining corpus size and investment returns, if funders focused on making material and sizable investment in communities, and dramatically increased the amounts they award, then social impact organizations and the communities they serve could more immediately and successfully address urgent needs and the bigger systemic issues creating those needs. It is of course understandable that some feel the need to reserve financial assets for a rainy day. And yet, it is also true that organizations are struggling today for the resources to support critical programs and services. Additional funds today could address so many unmet needs.

Fortunately, there are additional resources that funders can leverage toward social impact organization's work generally and technology success specifically. Putting technology to work for social impact realistically entails funders acknowledging and investing through all their assets and resources.

Utilize program-related investments (PRIs)[6] as viable and valuable options for funding social impact infrastructure like technology projects and systems. For many organizations, such technology projects as upgrading systems, migrating to more dynamic or integrated platforms, or even redesigning the website can require a significant up-front cost and result in increased revenue for the organization—through increased donations, or via the cost savings of scaled programs or removing duplicative tools or processes. Since PRIs, unlike grants, are time-bound loans with below-market-rate interest rates, they are a financially viable model for the organization. Also, since recipients pay back the loan, the PRI model also increases the collective assets available to the community when the funder redistributes the funds.

The amount of funds a foundation devotes to its social good mission, unfortunately, are often limited to grantmaking despite those accounting for less than 5% of assets annually. It's an unfortunate truth: some companies, portfolios, and systems in which foundations invest their endowment for the highest returns ultimately exacerbate the very social issues that the grantmaking side of the foundation is intended to address. Clara Miller is President Emerita of the Heron Foundation, which she led from 2011–2017. In June 2021, for *Nonprofit Quarterly*, she wrote:[7]

"But what were you doing before?"

A young man, standing at the back of a lecture hall in Michigan, posed this question after a presentation I made in 2011 when I was president of the Heron Foundation. I was explaining with gusto that Heron was aligning all its assets—100 percent of endowment capital—with its anti-poverty mission.

But he was unimpressed. He thought he was coming to hear about "cutting-edge philanthropy." And he learned that until recently, our supposedly innovative foundation wasn't even doing what he thought all foundations already did: directing all their financial capital toward their missions.

And if I had shared more, I likely would have impressed him even less. He would have learned that Heron was and has remained an outlier for 25 years,[8] and that the core business of endowed foundations is not mission-oriented; it is conventional investment management. And he would also have learned that foundations pay chief investment officers on average three times what chief executives make in salary, benefits, and bonuses. . . . [9]

The paradigm—the operating model, asset allocation, and culture—that segregates a foundation's core investing business from its more marginal philanthropic operation must be integrated, or real progress, too, will be unattainable.

In September 2021, John Palfrey, President of the MacArthur Foundation, announced that they would make this same kind of alignment between their mission and their assets: "The MacArthur Foundation works to create a more just, verdant, and peaceful world. One of our Big Bets seeks to support Climate Solutions through a coordinated strategy of grantmaking and impact investments. In line with these goals, we are committing to greater alignment between our endowment investments and our programmatic goals, mission, and values. Today we share that we are on a path to divesting from fossil fuels." [10] In the announcement posted on the MacArthur Foundation website and sent via email to constituents, John also acknowledged that "Foundations like MacArthur use massive tax-exempt wealth as the engine to provide grants for the public good. How we deploy our wealth through grants and impact investments makes a difference. How we invest and grow our endowment is important, too. I hasten to acknowledge there are some foundations and advocates who have been ahead of us and shown the way."

Commitment to a better world calls for funders aligning their resources with the work to build that world. An annual minimum IRS distribution cannot create the change we want to see, especially if remaining resources are invested in stocks and markets that directly harm communities, perpetuating the same issues so many are working to end.

Funding Tech to Be Developed for Social Impact

There are dozens and dozens of smart phone and computer applications that enable a user to browse and order food delivery or pickup from restaurants and grocery stores. At the other end of the spectrum, there are only a few applications that help a user find food pantries and other free food resources. Given that 42 million people in the United States experience food insecurity,[11] it's clear that technology development of this sort isn't aligned with areas of the most need.

This imbalance extends across the social impact sector as there are far more technology products developed for the nonprofit sector by for-profit entities rather than by nonprofits and community groups themselves. As discussed in chapter 4, many contributing factors create this reality. Of critical importance is that funding for new technologies for social impact is expected to fit into existing capitalist models that reward and even require tech companies to secure as many users as possible at any cost—often with the goal of selling the product to someone else. Funders can create the change they want to see by changing the way they resource technology development for social impact.

Fund for Specialization   In the social impact sector, there is no single model of social services, community support, or change making that would work for every situation, every geography, or even every issue area. We can't expect, then, for the same technology platforms and applications to benefit every use case and be deployed in every organization. Technical customization is not enough to bend a for-profit sales platform or a mass-market person-to-person communication app into something relevant and effective for social impact work. Similarly, a technical development priority to build only for the widest market reach will not provide the kind of nuanced solutions that make for truly effective social impact organizations.

We should not need every social service provider to use the same set of tools if the programs they offer, the services they deliver, and the communities they serve are different. Every arts organization does not need to use the same video conferencing tool to be successful. Technology should match the needs of organizations and communities, not be the shape to which organizations and communities need to conform.

If the goal is to build strengthened and empowered communities, then the tech must be relevant to those communities. That means building the right tools to support specific efforts. Note, however, that we can't expect fast results or immediate scaling from community-specific solutions; not all solutions can be universally adopted by all other nonprofits and community groups. With time and additional research and development, though, more broadly applicable solutions may be developed and deployed elsewhere. Long-term investment in community-centered technology development would enable everyone— funders, technologists, and social impact organizations—to use what works in one community and adapt it to be put to work in another, because that new version or application would benefit from the specialized and localized research and development already undertaken.

With 1.5 million nonprofits in the United States,[12] not including community groups without a 501(c)(3) IRS status and millions more around the world, building something that every social impact organization wants, finds appropriate, and adopts isn't an option. However, the fear that building technology that doesn't have a universal market means it is too niche is unfounded as the US nonprofit sector alone employs 10% of the nation's population with 11.4 million jobs.[13] A product that serves just 1% of the social impact organization staff in the United States serves 114,000 people in thousands of organizations, which themselves serve potentially millions of community members.

It is important to note that developing technologies to address more tailored needs and scenarios will require funders to commit to these projects for the long term. This is not an arena for the acquisition and consolidation of a technology company; specialized platforms and applications for social impact need to be maintained and supported over time, without organizations fearing that the products will disappear or become obsolete.

Funding the development of technology for social impact requires funding for specialization, embracing the reality that tools fit for specific purposes will have clearer paths to adoption by social impact organizations and thus will enable more positive outcomes. Flip the priority from the most people using a product to the most people benefiting from the technology used by social impact organizations.

Prioritize Proximity to Impact   In many ways Silicon Valley is seen as the best resource for building these specialized technologies, but in that approach is an inherent separation between those creating technology and those using it. For example, searching for the term "nonprofit" in the Google Play Store results in hits that suggest what social impact organizations need most is fundraising support. Although it is true that having more financial resources is beneficial, if we ask staff and community members what technologies would best help them fulfill their missions, their replies would naturally reveal needs more diverse than fundraising apps. Developers who build tech without the experience and perspective of the intended users produce tech based on assumptions, biases, and misaligned priorities—which helps no one.

Instead of creating technology "for" social impact needs, let's focus on creating technology "with and by" those working for social impact. Doing so calls for funding in a different way, such as funding social impact organizations as the lead developers. Funding social impact organizations to hire or work closely with developers situates the technology solutions in direct relationship to the issues and regions being addressed. It also creates a foundation for iteration and evolution of the technologies in context, where development staff can make changes and improvements as real-world use cases present new opportunities. Proximity to impact in this way means that many of the proven successful strategies for technology development—including rapid prototyping, deep user knowledge, and testing in the field—are a natural reality. It means better products enabling better outcomes for users.

Funding social impact organizations as the leaders and owners of technology solutions also creates new opportunities for the social impact organizations themselves to be the tech providers to other organizations, which would greatly reduce the expenses needed for adoption and marketing. Technology development housed inside a social impact organization, or coalition of organizations, presents earned revenue, shared revenue, and collective ownership models as viable opportunities for maintaining the products for longer-term use and scale.

Funders can best serve social impact organizations and initiatives by investing in technology solutions developed from a diversity of places and communities, because no single mission, community, or cause area could dictate a technology solution applicable across the sector.

Commit to Inclusion   Prioritizing proximity to impact connects directly into committing to inclusion. Whether technology development happens inside a social impact organization, in a technology company, or anywhere else, community members—those who will use or interact with the products, have their data stored in the products, or be served through the products' use—need to be included in the processes of designing, planning, building, and implementing them. The collection of barriers to participation in technology development today can be understood as systemic exclusion; that is, the priorities and values that influence how technology teams and projects approach their work rely on and reinforce exclusive access and knowledge. Counteracting this is the adoption of systemic inclusion, or a combination of new values and priorities, including those outlined in chapter 2, that clarify that technology development cannot be successful if community members aren't deeply part of the work. Participatory processes and trust with the community can be areas of valuable evaluation for funders when vetting both the social impact organizations and technology providers. Established processes, committees, and active engagement in collaborative work with and in the communities affected by the technology can be prerequisites to quality for funding to take on technology development.

To enable inclusive engagement, funding needs to be sufficient to provide equitable compensation to community members for their participation, as well as to provide staffing, processes, and communications that support diverse communities' full participation. Social impact organizations and communities engaged in their programs and services have many other areas of obligation that complicate their availability to work with the development team, including staff who care deeply about the product but have competing priorities and program timelines, and community members who are navigating jobs, services, school, and more. Funding a project adequately for inclusive development includes compensation for community members' participation in acknowledgment that their lived experience is valuable, especially when it isn't shared by members of the development team, and that their time is valuable.

Inclusion also applies to the speed at which technologies are designed and implemented, because only deep engagement with the community being served will produce effective products. Ample time to apply test-use feedback must be built into the schedule. This doesn't mean that technology projects focused on supporting social impact work need to take a long time, but goals for inclusion need to be the filters through which we evaluate how much time is needed.

Inclusion in technology development may also mean collaboration with other technology development teams or companies who have tried similar projects, built similar technology platforms, or have failed when attempting to address the same or similar social impact areas. We do not need to build new products from scratch for every new project to be valid or valued for funding. Embarking on a project without collaborative input could replicate failed attempts made by others working in similar social impact areas, making the investment far less effective or likely to be successful anyway.

Accelerate Experimentation   Another way in which the for-profit model doesn't translate to the nonprofit sector is the fact that funding of social impact organizations usually comes with the expectation that the venture must succeed. Grants are often structured in a way that disallows an iterative process of development that can surface new and different priorities from those originally outlined in the grant application—even though such a process is best suited to meeting community needs. Given that 70% of tech start-ups fail,[14] these expectations are clearly inappropriate. Little is gained by requiring technology development projects to soar on their first try. Conversely, if we expect iterative evolution, we gain the longer vision to get it right. This calls for funders investing at levels and with the flexibility that allows tech development to test, experiment, and innovate toward success. Just as we need space to imagine different futures, we also need space (and the funding that creates it) to imagine new and better technologies for our needs.

An investment in this kind of rethinking and experimentation for social impact technology is an investment in shared learning spaces. Instead of funding the next application or platform, fund technical learning communities from which the next application or platform can intentionally emerge. We learn more from failure when it can happen without stigma and in an environment invested in learning. A version that didn't work is only really a failure if we can't learn from it and build better in the next round. Collaborative learning and development offers opportunities for new technologies as well as for continued iterations, as the lessons from one project may inspire another.

Shared learning spaces are more than a stand-alone weekend hackathon. They are more than pro bono technologists putting in limited volunteer hours. Funding shared learning and experimentation of technology for social impact requires intention, commitment, and inclusive engagement. They need long-term support, dedicated coordination and documentation, and shared leadership by social impact organizations and the communities they support.

When that long-term support and collaboration does exist, shared learning spaces can be a fertile area for further growth and evolution of technology tools. As we've said, technology isn't going to be exactly right on the first try—but in shared learning spaces, community users, organizations, funders, technologists, and even policymakers can understand how they aren't working or meeting needs now, and they can continue to iterate on the technologies version after version, learning and reflecting each time, getting ever closer to the most valuable solution for the users. Mala Kumar from GitHub agrees that there's value in ensuring that these later iterations be able to emerge:[15]

> Everyone wants to fund the first thing. They want to say they funded a cool new innovation but they only funded year 1, they didn't fund years 2 and 3 when the application or tool could have been improved. So, the result is the app didn't work. But of course, it didn't work. What piece of technology works right away? Involving local communities is necessary, but it also just takes a lot of time to get it right and you aren't going to get it right in the first instance. And what is "right" exactly? Technology is always going to evolve. Long term institutional funding for tech for social good is necessary beyond iteration 1. We need more efforts to find what exists or has been tried and fund iterations 2, 3, and 4.

Regardless of the type of funder an organization or individual may be—from philanthropist to venture capitalist to major donor—the priorities for funding technology to be deployed for social impact are specialization, proximity to impact, inclusive processes, and experimentation. Every kind of funder can be a funder of technology for and in social impact work. In fact, every kind of funder should be a funder of technology for and in social impact work.

Developing New Models for Investment

At the risk of stating the obvious, the points discussed here do not align with the standard models of investment. Many of the funding models we have today—including private philanthropy, corporate philanthropy, venture capital, venture philanthropy, and even major donor fundraising—assume that the vast majority of the financial resources will be held outside of the community and the social impact organizations working to support that community. There is a consistent expectation of maximizing financial return—whether from the individual investments in projects or from the investment management of the centralized assets the foundation holds—at the expense of maximizing outcomes.

Just as we need to fund technology development that has the closest proximity to impact and the deepest relationships with the community, the allocation and management of funding for this work needs to move away from external groups and into funds, collectives, coops, or other resource management structures where the target communities are able to lead.

Concentration of resources should be within the community, not as a concentration of wealth by a few individuals and entities, even if those people and organizations claim to have a social benefit mission or commitment. So many of the divisions, challenges, and difficult dynamics of the social impact sector and the models for making change today are products of saviorism, taking a paternalistic view of charity. In addition, funding models for technology are inherently flawed, as they reinforce financial return over impact. Jenny Kassan, a business attorney and social entrepreneur, explains, "The venture capital model and ecosystem for funding technology businesses creates high levels of inequality in many ways, including who gets rich when companies are successful, who suffers when a company is not able to meet the growth imperative imposed by investors, and who even has access to this funding in the first place."[16]

Considering the illustration of systemic exclusion from chapter 1, barriers to relationships between funders and communities can be understood as both physical and operational, as Wilneida Negrón, a social entrepreneur, researcher, and public interest technologist, explains:[17]

> We are at a critical moment in time when we're increasingly examining the business models, company building practices, and revenue generation strategies which have supported the major tech companies of the past 20 years. As a result, this is also a period of experimentation around ownership structures, business and alternative financing models, and revenue streams. However, the challenge is cultivating the catalytic and patient capital that's needed to support the next generation of responsible company building founders, especially those trying to combine scale and growth with societal impact and/or accountability to a broader set of stakeholders, like workers, communities, environment, and consumers. The challenge for the field and investors, both private and philanthropic, is the need to work and learn together in order to identify best practices from investment models that blend philanthropic and private capital with an eye to maximizing the achievement of the overall mission of the next generation of companies via the provision of aligned capital. For example, philanthropy should seek to become less risk-averse and learn to manage the investment risk—whether real or perceived—that comes with investments in a new generation of tech companies, while private capital can be catalytic as long as investors understand the mission must be preserved. This will be a challenge for traditional investors who usually take big ownership stakes in enterprises and exert significant pressure on them. Venture capital investments, in particular, can push enterprises toward indiscriminate growth or a sale that may be inconsistent with the underlying mission of an enterprise.

If we want an equitable world, we cannot prioritize the hoarding of wealth, resources, and power by select individuals. What if we were to create and implement solutions for ensuring that communities and individuals have the resources they need to sustain their lives in their environments, maintain liberty within their experience, and pursue their version of happiness? What if we were instead to believe that we have the most power when we come together?

The good news is that there are some interesting and compelling examples of communities and funders working together in different ways today. We can push even further, building on their progress toward the equitable world that comes next—that could be next.

An example of an intentional investment model that uses values as the vetting criteria is Parity.[18] "Parity invests in technological innovation that preserves or protects our rights to privacy, security, and ethical use of emerging technologies such as Artificial Intelligence and Quantum Computing." The Parity team understands that as individuals learn more about digital platforms, internet policy, and the way their data can and is being used, often without their knowledge or informed consent, the more those individuals will migrate to different services, apps, or platforms that provide more control and protection. It is both a business case and a matter of ethics to invest only in companies committed to user rights, making the model one that can operate inside some of the systems we have today while bridging us forward to a better world.

With only 2% of investor funding in the United States and 10% globally going to start-ups founded by women, Women Who Tech looks to shift who receives the capital needed to build new technologies and to increase financial support for women, transgender, nonbinary, and gender nonconforming folks who are creating new tools. [19] Women Who Tech is a "nonprofit organization building a culture and inclusive economy to accelerate women tech entrepreneurs and close the funding gap." They facilitate collective fundraising that can be redirected into a diverse pool of founders working across industries, markets, and project types, including mobile apps, platforms, and companies working in health, food, legal aid, recruitment and hiring, and more. "If the tech sector wants to truly innovate, then investors will need to be more intentional about diversifying their portfolios and be more inclusive. It's time to tackle the gap in venture capital funding head on," says Allyson Kapin, founder of Women Who Tech. This isn't a system solution, of course, but an appropriate current intervention as we shift the funding environment. "I hope one day organizations like Women Who Tech won't have to exist because the tech and startup world will truly be diverse, equitable and supportive of women, especially women of color," explains Allyson. "But until that day comes, Women Who Tech will be on the frontlines standing up to make a lot more space for women founders and women in tech who have been historically overlooked."

When resources are invested in community for technology development—instead of invested in technologies that are then marketed to various communities—we are able to keep values and priorities closely aligned. Another example of community-driven technology development is May First Movement Technology, which "engages in building movements by advancing the strategic use and collective control of technology for local struggles, global transformation, and emancipation without borders." One might ask, Why would people use technology services from this group instead of from any manner of other major technology providers? Here's their answer:

> More than just a technology, the Internet is a massive network of people using computers to communicate with each other. It changes in size and character every second of the day as people log on and off and do what they log on to do. And it has a culture, a history, and a vitally important future.
>
> That culture is based on freedom of communication: a place where everyone with an opinion or a story can express it.

The history is one of collaboration: where every major function of the Internet is driven by software that is free, developed by large groups of volunteers working together, and maintained by teams of skilled volunteers, most of whom have never met personally.

And the future is one of social change. The Internet has already played a critical role in combatting disinformation, expressing new ideas, delivering truth, and bringing committed people together. It is among the social justice movement's most potent communications tools.

In short, [the internet is] ours, and we should be using and developing it to the fullest. That's why we're building May First Movement Technology.[20]

As a membership organization, May First members receive the level of hosting services and other technology support they could buy elsewhere, but they also have shared investment and ownership of the direction, priorities, and decisions of the organization. They have a values-aligned service provider who actively works to support shared goals. That centralizes the power, momentum, and resourcing within the community.

The tech that comes next will be funded in new ways, with deeper connection in the communities it affects and supports. To build a better world we all need to be part of shifting the way we fund both social impact work and the technology used in and developed for social impact.

QUESTIONS FOR WHAT'S NEXT

For social impact organizations, technology projects, and community initiatives, funding is often a critical resource that can determine if an effort is possible, how it can work, and who can be involved. Small amounts of funding spread out thinly misses the needs and reality that technology projects and social change require long-term support, space for learning and testing, and a systemically inclusive approach. Reimagining new ways of working together and resourcing the work of change requires we ask more questions of ourselves and those we engage with. Use the questions below to guide, instigate, and otherwise open up new conversations and ideas.

Social Impact Organizations

Questions for those working in and with social impact efforts to ask funders:

- It's important to us that we retain both oversight and control of our work. And while we will report what outcomes your funding would enable us to produce, that reporting will not be granular. Are you ready to provide funding while also respecting our methods?
- Can you support adequate funding to bring more development staff and teams into social impact organizations?
- What experience or history do you have with the communities we work with?
- How will you support us in honoring the self-determination of our program participants and community members?
- How do you respond to failure? Are you open to shared learning?

Technologists

Questions for those building technology for social impact to ask funders:

- Are you willing to provide enough funding for us to (a) hire team members from impacted communities, and (b) support their technical and professional development in this project?
- Are you ready to fund us with a long-term commitment so we can ensure we provide support, maintenance, and ongoing improvements after launch?
- How will you support us in retaining access to our intellectual property so we can continue to learn and use it elsewhere?

- What is your comfort level with slower return on investment so that we can be purposeful in engagement and development?
- Are you committed to funding for inclusive processes that include slower development timelines and compensation to participants?

Funders

Questions for those in positions to fund social impact and technology to ask of their peers:

- If you spent down the fund, how much faster could you meet your mission and accelerate impact in your funding region?
- What steps do you take to staff your organization inclusively?
- How are you investing in your staff's tech knowledge and capacity?
- How can we work together to create a pool of funding that is turned over for community ownership?
- How are you leveraging all of your organization's assets—beyond grants—in order to meet the mission?

Policymakers

Questions for those creating and enforcing policies around technology and social impact to ask funders:

- What policies or other legal mechanisms would most catalyze your institution to increase the amount of funding distributed?
- Can you commit to being part of policy accountability?
- What can we do to encourage your participation in public–private–community partnerships?
- How can we work together to extend initiatives toward accessibility and equity in your community?
- How are you working in cross-sector collaborations to surface priorities?

Communities

Questions for community members to ask funders:

- How do we build trust with you so that our solutions can be prioritized?
- It's important to us to influence who gets approval to work in our community. How can we partner with you on that?
- It's important to us that your strategic planning and portfolio priorities reflect the lived realities and needs of our community. How can we best share our priorities with you? How does our feedback factor into your definition and expectation of return on investment?
- Are you committed to funding solutions to work with groups that are not designated 501(c)(3) or another equivalent registered charity organization?
- It is important to us that we are engaged as early as possible. How will community engagement take place prior to decisions about what or whom to fund?

Chapter Six
Changing Laws and Policies

Policymaking is ultimately about effecting change for large groups of people; centering the communities most affected by potential policies in the policymaking processes is the only way we will create a more equitable world. Participation with the public in the design of policy allows policymakers to address all the issues the communities face—infrastructure, access to services, and more. Technology can support the flow of information throughout communities and between communities and policymakers. But what happens if communities don't have access to the technology? Or, what happens if the technology to which communities do have access causes confusion, disenfranchises people, or fails to protect them?

The policymaker that comes next must consider all these aspects in their role. They must insist on involving community members and social impact organizations in the policymaking process. They must make sure communities can access technology. They must understand how technology intersects with the issues they govern. They must require that the technology that touches society is secure, trustworthy, and not exploitative. It's a lot to manage, but by listening to their constituents, getting advice from experts, and effectively using technology themselves, policymakers can create rules and regulations that enable a thriving society.

In a world where regulation is scarce and there are no requirements to institute social checks and balances on the work of social impact organizations, however, the people who design technology are the de facto policymakers, the creators of social paradigms, and the deciders regarding who receives services and who doesn't. It's a weighty responsibility for technologists to carry alone—and it should not be this way.

Take, for example, the seemingly straightforward act of displaying ads on a social networking site. Algorithms, developed and implemented by technologists, now perform a portion of content moderation that previously was handled entirely by humans via physical mediums—such as print newspapers or even bulletin boards. One point in favor of such algorithms is the fact that, say, an ad for housing that explicitly states certain groups are unwelcome will be quickly removed from most sites. But what if advertisers want to target their ads with a bit more nuance? In 2019, the US Department of Housing accused Facebook of participating in housing discrimination. Facebook's ad practices, which allow for traditional market segmentation, easily lend themselves to discriminatory practices, since advertisers can restrict ads from being shown to groups who fall under the protections of the Fair Housing Act.[1]

Algorithms used on social networking sites often display the algorithm's best guess of what you want to see; this means you will often see what people similar to you are looking for and you won't see content that people different from you search for. And so, in the case of the Facebook example, if you are a Hispanic woman looking for a place to live, you may not see ads for apartment buildings that are overwhelmingly occupied by white residents—whether or not you would have voluntarily included or excluded that building in your search.

Individuals who make policies and plans for local, state, and federal governments—that is, policymakers—who have often spent their careers in the policymaking world, traditionally come from nontechnical backgrounds. This would not be a significant problem if society still operated as it did a century ago—before modern technology was so intertwined in how people live their lives and how policy is implemented. For example, given how poorly the 2010 Affordable Care Act rolled out in 2014, the policymakers who wrote the Act vividly realized the importance of ensuring that the technical design of healthcare.gov complemented the policymaking.

But this is not to say that all policymakers should also be technology experts; that would be unreasonable. Policymaking itself is a specialized skill that takes time and experience to refine. But policymakers must consider how technology can extend the impact of policy. The conversation about policymaking for what comes next must come from two angles: policy about technology, and technology in policymaking. The common factor in improving policymaking in both cases is strengthening the connection between policymakers and community members. To this end, it is important that policymakers proactively seek out technical expertise—and not just in corporate America, but also within grassroots advocacy organizations and other social impact organizations. Similarly, it is important that technologists learn how to simply and sincerely explain to policymakers the technology they develop. Without this collaborative spirit, policymakers and technologists will continue to talk past each other, and no useful or practicable policy will be developed. For another example, consider the issue of regulating encryption. Privacy advocates argue that encryption regulation protects consumers, whereas law enforcement argues that it thwarts lawful investigations. How can members of Congress be expected to regulate encryption when they struggle to understand its definition, let alone how it works?

Just as technology can be used to advance the missions of social impact organizations, technology can also be used to structure policymaking conversations in new ways. Technologists can inject new-to-policy design processes that consider how policies may be successfully technically implemented, as well as how to repeatedly learn and adjust based on testing and piloting designs.

Chapters 3, 4, and 5 discussed how individual roles within the social impact sector can embrace technology to facilitate conversations with community members and advance justice and equity missions. Each of these roles has significant power and agency to influence both their individual organization's work and the work of coalitions. However, to effect widespread systems change, policies, regulations, and laws must also change. Policymakers are uniquely positioned to adjust these levers, and they too can actively participate in building what comes next.

CASE STUDY 1: NATIONAL DIGITAL INCLUSION ALLIANCE

Angela Seifer is the Executive Director at the National Digital Inclusion Alliance. NDIA "is a unified voice for home broadband access, public broadband access, personal devices, and local technology training and support programs. NDIA is a community of digital inclusion practitioners and advocates. [They] work collaboratively to craft, identify, and disseminate financial and operational resources for digital inclusion programs while serving as a bridge to policymakers and the general public."[2] In 2019, NDIA joined conversations about the emerging Digital Equity Act—sponsored by Senator Patty Murray, Chair of the Senate Health, Education, Labor, and Pensions (HELP) Committee; Senator Rob Portman; and Senator Angus King—which "would help close the digital divide impacting communities across the nation."[3] The content of the Act built on previous digital equity policy work in Seattle, Washington. Fortunately, valuable policies can start at various levels; strong local- or state-level policies can be considered and modified at the federal level, thus serving as blueprints for policies to be implemented nationally. As such, the Seattle-area policy work to support comprehensive interventions for digital divides served to inform how a national policy could similarly address the complexity of the issues. NDIA joined ongoing conversations about what would become the Digital Equity Act at the request of staffers in Senator Murray's office, who sought input from a number of organizations and community leaders for insight into how to ensure that the policy was both balanced and representative of best practices.

NDIA, as a coalition and policy organization, has a number of social impact organizations as members. These organizations are the community leaders on the ground teaching folks to use the internet, getting devices for community members, signing up for or building high-speed internet, and more. By collaborating with these organizations and individuals, NDIA is able to gather broad examples and understanding from communities across the United States, advocate on behalf of organizations and individuals regarding the challenges they face, and adjust advocacy efforts based on any changing circumstances on the ground. In essence, NDIA takes their coalition members' expertise and experiences to the policymakers so that they can understand the lives and challenges of their constituents.

Angela sees the Digital Equity Act as a valuable example of what policy could be: "The uniqueness of the Digital Equity Act is that it is holistic in nature. It goes after all the barriers. It's not just about devices, the internet connection, or digital literacy. Those things tend to get put into buckets, and when there has been funding they are funded separately. This is the first time we have a holistic approach—considering all those things are important."[4] How did this version of this particular bill come to reflect the lessons communities had learned? It started with information sharing among committees and policymakers.

Senator Murray's office, Angela reports, sought input and opinions from NDIA and other advocacy organizations. "They didn't *need* to do this, but they did"—and because they did they were able to learn from previous policy attempts to address digital equity around the country. With prior policies, funds earmarked for digital inclusion "were separated, and therefore could only go so far." NDIA coalition members had seen that when funds had to be spent purely for workforce or health or connectedness, access to digital technologies only marginally improved individuals' quality of life. "People don't only use the internet to find a job, then decide they don't need to use the internet to email or text family and friends," Angela noted. A holistic funding strategy enshrined in a holistic policy would give communities a better chance to truly bridge the digital divide.

The information sharing did not only go from social impact organizations to policymakers; information also flowed back to the social impact organizations. Angela described the education process that NDIA coalition members underwent as they worked with policymakers on the Digital Equity Act. Witnessing a policymaker saying, "I would love to do that, but . . ." allowed NDIA members to turn the interaction into a teachable moment. NDIA members would then ask, "What are the laws and limitations of that particular government agency in which we want to effect change? What are the barriers and restrictions we need to work within?" With this understanding, NDIA members could navigate the particular laws and policies currently governing particular operations, and change their information sharing with policymakers based on this understanding.[5]

After years of work, in 2021, the Digital Equity Act was passed as part of the bipartisan Infrastructure Investment and Jobs Act. The bill created out of the listening and learning among policymakers and community organizations "aims to address these access gaps by encouraging the creation and implementation of comprehensive digital equity plans in all 50 states, DC, and Puerto Rico, [as well as by] supporting digital inclusion projects undertaken by groups, coalitions, and/or communities of interest. With this support, we can further our efforts to bridge the digital divide."[6] The work of NDIA and other organizations to gather and amplify the voices of communities, educate policymakers on the issues, and learn about the limitations of existing laws and authorities led policymakers to write and pass a bill that has the ability to have a positive impact on lives and increase connectedness in new, more comprehensive ways.

CASE STUDY 2: RURAL COMMUNITY ASSISTANCE PARTNERSHIP

Nathan Ohle began his tenure as CEO of the Rural Community Assistance Partnership (RCAP) in 2017. From the start he was curious about, among many issues, how effectively RCAP used technology to support its operations and its membership. RCAP is a national non-profit focused on securing and maintaining access to water and economic development for rural communities across the country; it is the "national network of non-profit organizations working to provide technical assistance, training, resources, and support to rural communities across the United States, tribal lands, and US territories. [Its] federal programs and organizational interests are maintained in the national office in Washington, DC, while state and regional programs and field work are managed through six regional offices."[7]

He opted to partner with New America's Public Interest Technology team to conduct a sprint—a short but intensive and focused effort to review the current state of affairs and make recommendations to strengthen structures, systems, and technology. The sprint was needed, Nathan felt, so RCAP could learn how they might use technology to drive positive change; they would use the ground truth they discovered to come up with a strategy around what capacities RCAP needed in the work to fill any revealed gaps and set up for future operations. A month later, the sprint team had delivered a report with recommendations about the type of technical talent the organization should hire, the specific technology products that could be acquired, and more.

Since the RCAP/New America Public Interest Tech partnership was successful, the teams looked for additional ways to collaborate. In particular, Nathan had observed how well the technologists had structured the conversations within the organization. Nathan (a former policymaker himself) and the New America Public Interest Tech team (also composed of former policymakers) wanted to test how tech tools and methods—which could improve the internal workings of organizations—could also improve the policymaking process.

Around the same time, the 2018 Farm Bill was being drafted using traditional, incremental, policymaking processes. The Farm Bill is "a package of legislation passed roughly once every five years that has a tremendous impact on farming livelihoods, how food is grown, and what kinds of foods are grown." It covers "programs ranging from crop insurance for farmers to healthy food access for low-income families, from beginning farmer training to support for sustainable farming practices."[8] The team asked themselves: Are there new, innovative ideas that they should seed with policymakers now, as opposed to waiting to see what the House and Senate committees come back with?

The group decided to convene an Innovation Summit, a daylong event with "a coalition of rural community advocates, nonprofit leaders, and technologists to try out new methods of policy creation."[9] A number of technologists were identified to structure and facilitate the day. They would use a variety of tools common to inclusive tech development processes to bring to this policy brainstorming session the ability to include a number of diverse perspectives, to distribute power in decision making, and to develop prototypes. As Nathan recalls, "Technologists helped structure how to set up the day, how to drive thinking in new, innovative ways, and how to drive conversation after the Summit with people who were bought into the concepts discussed."

Over the course of the Innovation Summit, the large group, with representatives from multiple communities, came up with ideas for seven programs. Following the Summit, leaders of the group held smaller conversations to determine which idea had the most support and would best serve the needs of the communities the Summit participants represented. Taking part in the policymaking process, Nathan emphasizes, is made more effective when social impact organizations can build a coalition and advocate to policymakers with one voice. Accordingly, "We asked folks to go as a coalition to the Hill, and then took a subset of the group to speak with staff members on the Senate and House Agriculture Committees."[10]

During their conversations with staff members, the small, representative coalition provided an outline for a program that evolved into the Rural Innovation Stronger Economy (RISE) grant program. They answered questions from the policymakers and described how a new, innovative program would truly have an impact on the lives and livelihoods of members of rural communities across the country. In response, policymakers shared their knowledge about which levers could not be pulled—such as when a particular agency lacked authority to make a change, or when current laws or regulations would prohibit the implementation of parts of the proposal.

Policymakers finalized the RISE grant program details and continued the legislative process. In December 2019, the Farm Bill was signed into law; the RISE grant program "offers grant assistance to create and augment high-wage jobs, accelerate the formation of new businesses, support industry clusters, and maximize the use of local productive assets in eligible low-income rural areas."[11] What started from conversations among social impact leaders, rural community members, and technologists—using key techniques from social impact technologists—ended up as a new program managed by the federal government.

INSIDE THE PRACTICE OF CHANGE

Taken together, these two case studies describe the spectrum of work that policymakers must tackle: policy about technology and technology in policymaking. This spectrum applies to the universe of policymakers—elected officials, their aides, and their staffers—at federal, state, and local levels of government. A common factor in both the NDIA and RCAP work, reflected in the Digital Equity Act and the Farm Bill, was the creation of coalitions. In both cases, the power of including individuals with community expertise helped organizations to both learn from each other and prioritize interests. A second common factor was the importance of information sharing, communication, and accountability. Social impact organizations educated policymakers on community priorities, and policymakers educated social impact organizations on the confines of policy. A third common factor was the inclusion of technical expertise, although it looked different in each case. In the NDIA case study, policymakers benefited from hearing how the technology affected lives and how individuals needed to use the technology. In the RCAP example, the policy design process benefited from technical design thinking from the start.

At no point, however, was either group expected to have expert-level knowledge of the other players' constraints; rather, the ongoing efforts to center community challenges led to productive policymaking. Public interest technologist and cybersecurity policy expert Maurice Turner offers this advice to social impact organizations interested in affecting policy: "Treat policymakers as though they are people. They are people. If you are comfortable talking to people, then you can be comfortable talking to policymakers."[12] The reverse is also true: policymakers must also talk to communities and social impact organizations as though they are people. The policies and laws created provide a clear path for accountability between policymakers and communities. As with social impact organizations, technologists, and funding entities, policymakers must have conversations that center the community perspective in order to build what comes next.

Creating Policy About Technology

There are many opportunities to improve policy about technology, spanning the ways technology is developed, the ways people gain access to technology, and the ways technology is regulated. While it may seem that technology is changing every day, there's no reason policymakers cannot work with social impact organizations, technologists, funders, and communities to proactively and intentionally create policies and policy frameworks that serve to provide security and protection for all users.

Increase Access for Individuals   One of the biggest challenges today is simply ensuring that people have access to the technology they want and need, whether to connect with other people, organizations, businesses, services, or government agencies. People need access to technology not only to inform their lives, but also to communicate with their respective policymakers. Unfortunately, the digital divide—the gap between the people who do and do not have access to computers and the internet—leaves many people unable to participate in basic transactions. As Dr. Nicol Turner Lee writes, "Already facing diminished life chances, people with lower incomes, people of color, the elderly, and foreign-born migrants in rural areas run the risk of being on the wrong side of the digital divide that further exacerbates their economic, social, and political marginalization."[13] In some communities, residents resort to frequenting fast-food restaurants—to access their Wi-Fi services. Stop-gap measures such as these demonstrate the desire for connectivity, and the failure to provide it.

Digital redlining is the lack of availability of broadband access in particular communities. In 2017, a mapping analysis of Federal Communications Commission (FCC) broadband availability data revealed "that AT&T has systematically discriminated against lower-income Cleveland neighborhoods in its deployment of home Internet and video technologies over the past decade" by not extending the necessary technical infrastructure to the majority of Cleveland Census blocks where poverty rates were about 35%.[14] AT&T responded to this particular report by claiming they continuously invest in expanding services and enhancing speeds, and that they were in the process of conducting "technology trials over fixed wireless point-to-point milli-meter wave and G.fast technologies to deliver greater speeds and efficiencies within [their] copper and fiber networks.[15] Regardless of the intent in Cleveland, the reality remains that a significant percentage of neighborhoods in the United States lack access to high-speed internet, and policymakers have begun to take note. The proposed Anti-Digital Redlining Act of 2021 "would require the FCC to investigate whether internet service providers have discriminatory practices based on income, race, color, religion, national origin, and other factors within a geographic area."[16] After hearing the outcry of social impact organizations and understanding the tools available, policymakers are taking action.

Much of the problem results from the lack of significant and sustained efforts to increase broadband access, which is the primary way people access the internet with enough strength to take advantage of the technology that powers individual websites and programs. Fortunately, there are policies such as the Broadband Emergency Benefit, which provides "a discount of up to $50 per month towards broadband service for eligible households and up to $75 per month for households on qualifying Tribal lands."[17] But, though such policies are useful, they, like WiFi access in the parking lots of restaurants, are still only temporary band-aid solutions to a much bigger problem.

When broadband networks are built, it is important to maintain both the networks and access to the networks so they reliably provide the speed needed for efficient use. Funding must be provided for this, and policymakers have the authority to provide that funding.

A second major challenge of providing access to technology is ensuring that people continue to have agency over their lives. As more of our daily interactions are facilitated by technology, questions emerge around access to and ownership of our information.

It's important to recognize that lax security and privacy practices with technologies can, and often do, translate to real, even physical harm. For example, the SpyFone app, supposedly intended as a means for parents to monitor their kids' online activities and location, allowed "stalkers and domestic abusers to stealthily track the potential targets of their violence." The resulting crimes the app enabled led the Federal Trade Commission (FTC) to ban the company and its CEO from the surveillance business in September 2021.[18] We must examine how we can shift policymaking so as to better protect consumers.

We also have to explore the ways that institutions and communities can collaborate so as to design an environment that allows folks to create and thrive safely. To change systems—the very systems that so many social impact organizations fight against or try to work around—we must change policies. One way to navigate this is through advocacy organizations leading coalitions that speak directly with policymakers. Another option is the creation of public–private partnerships, which bring together resources and talents across multiple sectors to deliver services. Well-executed public–private partnerships can advance many of the goals of social impact organizations. In 2010, for example, the Gateway Arch Park Foundation partnered with the City of St. Louis and St. Louis County to renovate the Gateway Arch and increase visitor access. This public–private partnership "raised $250 million in private funding, and Great Rivers Greenway oversaw a publicly approved sales tax . . . that raised an additional $86 million for the project," which ultimately "led to a 30% increase in attendance."[19]

Part of what made the Digital Equity Act, discussed in the NDIA case study, so powerful was that it translated into policy the learning that a single intervention is not sufficient to solve deep-rooted, systemic problems. Policymakers can bring together a wide range of options to find solutions for the challenges communities articulate.

Make Proactive Policy About Technology   As the general public's understanding of how technology affects their lives increases, so does the general public's curiosity about how technology companies make decisions about marketing to or profiting from consumers—and about whether companies learn from the mistakes of their unpopular actions. Consequently, the calls for tech companies and technology to be regulated have increased over the past decade. Many consumers seek greater protection, wondering if tech companies follow them online or listen in to their conversations. Others resent being manipulated into engaging with online platforms or into purchasing decisions due to the intentional design practices of tech companies. Many wonder how privacy and security translate in a digital world. Is it possible to violate someone's sense of digital privacy and security? Should the government have the ability to gain access to our every move and communication? As Maurice Turner succinctly puts it, "Privacy and data protection are human rights."[20]

Increased awareness, combined with the years of research performed in many tech- and society-related academic programs, advocacy organizations, and civil society groups, has led to increased demand for regulating big tech. Articles such as "Tech Firms Need More Regulation,"[21] "Big Tech Says It Wants Government to Regulate AI. Here's Why,"[22] and "The World Wants More Tech Regulation"[23] have dotted the headlines over the past years. Even a *Harvard Business Review* piece entitled "How More Regulation for U.S. Tech Could Backfire" includes the statement, "Of course, nobody thinks technology companies should be left unregulated."[24] The true question, then, is who should do the regulating, and when?

Two particular government agencies are already set up to protect consumers and are well positioned for regulating information flow through technology: the FCC and the FTC can hold companies accountable for the harms they inflict on consumers. The FCC is responsible for implementing and enforcing communications laws and regulations. Some of its activities include "promoting competition, innovation and investment in broadband services and facilities" and "supporting the nation's economy by ensuring an appropriate competitive framework for the unfolding of the communications revolution."[25] The FTC protects consumers and promotes competition; it can "conduct investigations, sue companies and people that violate the law, develop rules to ensure a vibrant marketplace, and educate consumers and businesses about their rights and responsibilities."[26]

We've already seen examples of these two agencies at work—in the earlier discussions of SpyFone example and the Emergency Broadband Credit. These agencies, especially, must have sufficient technology expertise to interpret regulations around communications—including internet communications, antitrust practices, and consumer protection practices—under the lens of technology design and implementation. Policymakers can apply lessons already proven by the FCC and FTC to other policymaking bodies and government agencies.

It's no secret that most lawmakers do not have a deep understanding of the inner workings of technology. In congressional hearings, policymakers have been infamously confused and misinformed about how big tech companies function, even how the heavily used technologies of social media actually work, and what can't be done through technology. Unfortunately, that policymakers would be out of touch is somewhat by design. The traditional, siloed nature of policymaking has created individuals who don't understand, for example, the underlying effects of the ways technology dictates who can access broadband services, or how social media platforms influence teenagers' self-esteem, or how the location of tech factories can build up or destroy entire communities.

Policymakers are not technologists, by and large; they don't usually come from the tech world. But because of technology's impact on so much of people's lives, policymaking bodies must make decisions about its regulation—and so it is imperative that policymakers consult with tech advisers. They need to listen to the right people—not just to companies who can afford the time and access. In reality, policymakers must turn to those with not only technical expertise, but with ethical and societal expertise as well. The big tech companies have a number of legislative affairs and policy employees who are more than willing to educate lawmakers on their technology and on what regulation, if any, would help the tech industry. It is equally important, however, for policymakers to hear from privacy advocates and security experts and community members who use and are subject to the decisions of tech companies. It should be just as important for policymakers to hear how a security breach caused a consumer to lose their life savings. Or how people of color can experience race-based job discrimination even before getting an interview—because, as a Harvard study found, Google searches including African American–sounding names "are more likely to produce ads related to criminal activity."[27] Ready to provide some much-needed insight are organizations such as Upturn, which sets out to "drive policy outcomes and spark debate through reports, scholarly articles, regulatory comments, [and] direct advocacy efforts together with coalition allies."[28]

Policymaking also doesn't have to be just about cleaning things up or fixing things—it could be about articulating the pathways we want technology to follow in order to best serve those who use it. What's important is that communication takes place, that community members can express their concerns to their elected officials, sharing, "I need a more affordable option for this service" or "We need faster internet speeds" or "I need to be able to move my data off your system." Policymakers can listen to community members, then work with technologists to translate those needs into policies that will enable the related technologies to be built. For example, this process would turn a community's desire for more affordable internet access into legislation that allows for funding to be unlocked for the creation of new networks. In fact, this process played out in the creation of the 2021 Digital Equity Act, and funding was made available for local communities to find and build solutions they need—even outside of the traditional providers such as Verizon and Comcast.

We can't yet know all the ways technology will evolve. We do know that we need frameworks to allow people to be securely in charge of their data and protected from harm. Policymakers can partner with technologists and community members today to create guidelines that allow for innovation and creation while also preserving individuals' rights.

Using Technology in Policymaking

There are many ways for policymakers to encourage more thoughtful technology into policymaking. Although we can easily contact elected officials today, imagine, for example, there being a tool to increase trust, transparency, and accountability between policymakers and the communities they serve. Policymakers, social impact organizations, and community members can all use well-designed technology to access information to make data-driven decisions. Technology can then be used to implement policy decisions, such as those concerning delivering benefits, keeping people safe, and interacting with government agencies.

Technology Tools and Practices Can Be Used to Facilitate Policymaking

A primary goal of using technology in policymaking is to support closer communication between policymakers and constituents. Facilitating person-to-person conversations, sharing of data between different technical programs and applications, and guiding decision-making processes are all possibilities for redesigning policymaking for the twenty-first century.

Policymakers can learn a lot from technologists, and then apply those lessons to the process of policymaking. In 2019, Nathan Ohle and Cecilia Muñoz wrote, "Technologists, including user experience designers, computer scientists, and product managers, care deeply about how their products look and feel. They aren't afraid to make imperfect first versions, test them in batches, find the flaws, and iterate with new ideas. The process for creating new tech products is agile and collaborative—the exact opposite of the way most policy is made."[29] But it is possible to create policies that meet real needs. In the creation of the RISE Program that ended up in the Farm Bill (in Case Study 2, earlier), we saw how viable policy emerged from collaborative conversations between the community and social impact organizations that focused on identifying what programming, funding, and functionality would improve their lives.

To address the current lack of widely used technical tools for policymaking, let's encourage development of tools for gathering and assessing input in the policymaking process. Take, for example, the Mobility Data Specification (MDS). This digital tool "helps cities to better manage transportation in the public right of way. MDS standardizes communication and data-sharing between cities and private mobility providers, such as e-scooter and bike share companies."[30] By creating a digital platform that allows for the easy sharing of historical and real-time transportation data, cities are able to more easily track the use and efficiency of mobility programs and service providers. They can then quickly make policy decisions that reflect the newest information. As of late 2021, more than 130 cities around the world are using MDS—from Detroit, Michigan, to Bogotá, Colombia, to Ulm, Germany.

When policies have been clearly defined but may still be difficult to access, products developed by social impact organizations can help. For example, City Tech's Civic User Testing group (CUTgroup) "is a 1,600+ member civic engagement program that invites Chicago residents to contribute to emerging technology while providing public, private, and social sector partners with feedback to improve product design and deployment."[31] The group is mobilized for testing civic and government-related products. As we consider ways that technology can support policymaking, we must consider how to make the technology services that expand the inclusiveness and responsiveness of government services to communities.

Technology can also be used to empower policymakers and community members to view information in easily consumable ways, serving as a basis for decision making about policies and life decisions. Broadly distributing information is a way to ensure that policymakers and community members are making decisions from a common starting point, as well as to increase communities' abilities for self-determination. In 2020, as the COVID pandemic raged, communities and policymakers struggled to grasp the situation; information did not flow to inform conversations or decisions. Strategic use of coalitions and technology helps support decision making by policymakers—and community members. As Dr. Anjali Tripathi, creator of Los Angeles' COVID-19 vaccination dashboard and member of the Los Angeles County Department of Public Health's COVID-19 Data and Epidemiology Team writes,

> COVID-19 has tested our ability to rapidly transform large volumes of data into actionable information for communities. Working with the vaccination data for a population of over 10 million (America's largest county), we created a dashboard that—like a car dashboard—distills information into at-a-glance statistics and visualizations needed for tracking progress, identifying disparities, and taking action in real time.
>
> On its own, a single statistic for the number of people vaccinated or a table of geospatial data can be hard to interpret. However, a map of residents vaccinated by neighborhood quickly highlights communities that are lagging. Coupled with a time slider and graphs over time, these visualizations enable one to assess progress and the success of policy interventions, as well as provide forecasts for policy planning. It's amazing to see how providing data in context, for example showing how one city compares to others (such as neighboring cities or those of equivalent population sizes), incites self-motivated action.
>
> We carefully constructed our user interface, selected metrics, and disaggregated data to accessibly tell a story that would motivate action. Coupled with full open datasets available for download, our data dashboard has become a key self-service tool for a range of users—from academics and journalists to non-profit and government users. Our dashboard has powered other visualization and data efforts, including those for the Mayor's office of the City of Los Angeles, school districts, even other departments within the County of Los Angeles, such as the Department

of Health Services. The public facing website not only broke down silos affecting data sharing across government, it has been a key driver of policy action. It has been used to deploy mobile vaccination clinics and design more effective, targeted outreach (for example body shop and church vaccination events) in communities of color, with high rates of vaccine hesitancy. By making the data accessible, disaggregated by key demographics, and offering it in a near real-time, reliable and understandable format, our data dashboard has provided a key example of how data enables better outcomes, even in challenging quickly changing situations like a pandemic.[32]

With all of these interventions, a continually open line of communication is key. Communities and social impact organizations must be able to count on continued engagement with policymakers, whether through traditional media or through consistently used technologies.

Technical Decisions Can Affect the Adoption of and Compliance with Policy   It's also essential for policymakers to consider the technical implementation of the policies they create—especially supporting tools and systems that enable people to access the services they are legally entitled to. The importance of this approach can be seen in a stunning example.

In 2018, Arkansas became the first state to implement a Trump Administration policy that required Medicaid recipients to prove they were gainfully employed. But the only way for affected residents to report their compliance was via an online portal—despite the fact that Arkansas has the nation's lowest rate of household internet access. Six months into this experiment, nearly 20,000 people (more than 20% of those affected by the new rules) had lost health insurance coverage. Responding to public outcry, the state eventually established a telephone portal via which recipients could report their employment—except both the phone line and the website "close" at 9:00 each night, reopening at 7:00 the next morning.[33]

(Shockingly, this is not the only government website to have regular business hours.) These actions make it hard to imagine that the State of Arkansas actually wanted its least privileged citizens to receive their legally granted, potentially lifesaving health care benefits.

New Models for Policymaking

If we can't expect policymakers to become experts on technology, the next best thing is to bring technologists alongside policymakers. The TechCongress Fellowship aims to do just that—placing talented technologists in the policymaking halls of Capitol Hill for a limited term. This innovation had its beginnings in 2013, when founder Travis Moore was a Hill staffer. As a nontechnologist, he recognized that he needed support in advising his boss on how to vote on a particular bill. He shares: "I found there weren't staff on Capitol Hill with the necessary tech expertise to help me. As a result, I went outside the building, to a tech company lobbyist, for advice."[34]

In just a few years, TechCongress has proven that technologists working with policymakers can develop better tech-relevant policy; in a way, these technologists become policymakers themselves. Their successes include "changing defense procurement rules to allow startups to better compete for contracts and support our servicemembers; helping draft the House Judiciary Committee's Antitrust Subcommittee report on tech monopolies; issuing House Modernization Committee's recommendations to make Congress more effective, efficient and transparent; and passing the OPEN Government Data Act into law."[35] TechCongress now represents one pathway for technologists to provide impartial information on technology topics to policymakers. This model could be expanded at the federal level as well as modified and adopted for local city councils, for county commissions, for state-level governing bodies, and more.

Another example involves the United States Digital Service (USDS). Although now nearly a decade old, the USDS was created to better connect technology to policy development and implementation—both outside the legislative bodies and inside the government agencies that manage resources, regulate businesses, and generally administer specific government functions. The USDS model recognizes that policymakers may not know exactly what technology is needed to support specific policies, and so it brings in advanced technologists to work alongside policymakers.

USDS partnered with the Centers for Medicare and Medicaid Services to develop applications that "help give beneficiaries and their providers a 360-degree view of past diagnoses, procedures, and medications. Instead of forcing patients to recall and retell their entire medical history at each visit, providers can use Medicare claims information to confirm a patient's understanding of their medical history, fill in gaps in care, and improve patient safety."[36] Another USDS team partnered with the Veterans Affairs to "build a tool that guides users through nine questions and provides individualized results based on their responses. The customized plain language offers clear, step-by-step guidance on how a Veteran could present a strong application to upgrade their discharge status."[37] This is a lesson for all of us: never underestimate the power of replacing legalese and government speak with clear language that community members can understand and navigate! The digital service model started at the federal level in the United States has since expanded; there are now digital service agencies and practices being applied at state and local levels in the States as well as in countries around the world. Once again we see that broadening the participants in the policymaking process beyond traditional policy-only individuals leads to the development of effective solutions. Interestingly, though, the USDS has also found, again and again, that sometimes the better choice has been to intentionally *not* use technology—and to instead focus on administrative practices, process redesign, and community building.

So, yes, while it is necessary to expand traditional policymaking processes to include technologists in the design and implementation—that approach is also insufficient for creating the policies that must come next. Though policymakers have a lot to do within the policymaking process, they can also encourage others to invest in the policymaking process. Laura Manley, Executive Director of the Harvard Kennedy School's Shorenstein Center, says: "I often hear that policymakers just need to understand technology better. While that is true in many ways, it's not just up to non-technical folks to understand tech better. It's also up to technologists to understand policy and societal considerations better in their initial design, testing, and deployment."[38] Thus, even as more guardrails are put in place to preserve human rights, technologists will still maintain some power over policies as they are writing code.

Laura continues by acknowledging, "There are leverage points throughout all stages of a technology's development that should be considered—instead of only thinking about training for scientists and technologists at the beginning, or [about] regulation once it's out in the world. More time should be spent evaluating places like (1) basic and applied science grant requirements for inclusion, ethics, and testing or (2) the early stage investment process, and what due diligence [has actually been] considered." In other words, policymakers must appreciate that protections for individuals need to be built in from the start; waiting until the end of the technology development process to examine ethics and inclusion is simply waiting too long.

It's not just technologists who should educate themselves about the current realities of policymaking; traditional social impact organizations and advocacy groups must do the same, and policymakers should ask these organizations how technology effects their mission. The Leadership Conference on Civil and Human Rights is an example of a long-lasting and well-respected civil organization that has accepted that they cannot fully advocate for their mission without accounting for the many ways technology can advance or hinder their communities.

The Leadership Conference has embraced technology—not just by having an accessible, informative, user-friendly website that enables people to easily contact the relevant policymakers, but also by identifying some of the technology issues and policies that disproportionately affect their areas of concern. For example, the Leadership Conference has participated in or led coalitions to push the Census Bureau to ensure the 2020 Census would be conducted in a technically secure and accessible manner—and to get various levels of government to recognize the disproportionate effects that facial recognition technology has in policing.

In previous chapters we discussed the importance of intentionally designing technology for historically overlooked and excluded communities. The same must hold true for the policymaking community. As we create new models for policymaking, we must ensure that people of different backgrounds are able to contribute—as policymakers, as technologists, as social impact organizational leaders, and as community members. The particular issue of diversity, however, cannot be seen as an afterthought or a check-the-box exercise at the end of the process. As Arpitha Peteru and Sabrina Hersi Issa define as the first systemic inclusion principle: "How you create informs what you create."[39] At the point when decision-making tables are populated it's important to ask who is missing and what perspective isn't being represented, and then add someone who can speak to the nuances of this perspective.

Of course, it's important to also design policies inclusively; it's insufficient to design policies or implement technology that works for only most of the population—such a situation should be inadmissible as well. Arpitha Peteru and Sabrina Hersi Issa go on to point out, "There is an intrinsic relationship between online agency and offline power-building in the fight for justice and equity. But in an era when everyday existence in democratic and public life is facilitated by technology, online and offline states are not a binary. Digital devices, tools, and platforms fall across a continuum of unequal, inconsistent, and outsized power dynamics."[40]

Disinformation and misinformation are real threats to the policy-making process, and so one of policymakers' biggest challenges in the coming years will be the fight to find what is true. Case in point: the Facebook/Cambridge Analytica scandal. In the 2010s, the British political consulting firm Cambridge Analytica collected data from Facebook users without their consent; this information was then provided to the Ted Cruz and Donald Trump political campaigns, which in turn used the information to target Facebook users for political advertising. Despite Facebook's stated efforts to combat the widespread disinformation and misinformation on its platforms, users can still see and be swayed by inaccurate information on politics, global warming, the COVID-19 vaccine, and nearly any other subject. (Note that although Facebook is frequently cited as an offender in allowing the spread of disinformation and misinformation, it is by far not the only platform where this takes place; any information-sharing platform that provides analysis based on user data is vulnerable to this phenomenon.)

Much of the conversation about combating misinformation and disinformation centers around the general public; however, policymakers themselves are equally susceptible—with much more dangerous consequences. One simply cannot make solid policies if one bases decisions on inaccurate information. Fortunately, policymakers can fight the misinformation and disinformation they will inevitably be exposed to by verifying sources, sponsoring in-person discussions by holding community meetings, and providing community members and social impact organizations with opportunities to interact with decision makers in their local government.

Data, security, privacy laws, and policies are shifting the landscape for organizations and tech companies, and this trend will continue in the coming years. As non-tech businesses have learned, to operate in a global world they must understand and design processes around the regulations of the countries in which they work. Digital technologies are subject to the same constraints: technology regulations in one location may have ripple effects for technology companies doing businesses in multiple locations.

As we shift policymaking outside of its traditional silos and into the more open and connected world, relationships will be key. Relationships are how technologists effectively partner with traditional policymakers, and how communities and social impact organizations organize and build coalitions. Brandon Forester, the National Organizer for Internet Rights and Platform Accountability at MediaJustice, has wise advice about how to address this important shift: "Recognize that shifts don't happen overnight, and all coalition members don't need to be of one accord all the time."[41] Similarly, every potential unknown factor cannot be accounted for through communication and coalitions. Tech companies, for example, may not cite a need to protect proprietary information and not share how their technology works. This shift is toward a new process for policymaking, more than a one-time solution or single policy itself. Policymaking that supports a more equitable world will need to be a continual process of engagement, learning, and making change together.

QUESTIONS FOR WHAT'S NEXT

The opportunities for improvement in both policymaking about technology and the use of technology in policymaking rely on better understanding of how technology reflects policy and of how security and privacy manifest in technology systems—as well as understanding how best to center communities' needs and perspectives in policy creation. Policymakers must do a better job of requesting information from the full spectrum of their constituents—individuals, organizations, and companies. They should proactively seek to be educated on a broad range of technologies by social impact organizations and technologists, alongside their more traditional big-tech technology companies. To many social impact organizations, working on policy change can seem superfluous to or distracting from achieving their mission; however, policymakers should proactively ask these organizations to engage in the policymaking process so that we can change systems together. By empowering communities in the policymaking process, we can allow communities to identify tools or techniques that unnecessarily restrict their lives and livelihoods. The following questions can help start and advance conversations with policymakers to secure all these important goals.

Social Impact Organizations

Questions for those working in and with social impact efforts to ask policymakers:

- It's important to us that you fully understand the issues we know about and the priorities of the communities who are part of our work. How do we best educate you on those points?
- How do you help us navigate policymaking systems to ensure our efforts are successful? How will you help us know to engage and when?
- What have been successful strategies for organizations and communities advocating for new policies?
- Can you describe who and what influences your policies?
- How can we better work together on proactive policies that enable as many people and organizations as possible to be part of change-making work?

Technologists

Questions for those building technology for social impact to ask policymakers:

- How can we proactively understand current and forthcoming policy decisions? How can we help inform definitions within upcoming policies intentionally to ensure community adoption and protection?

- How can we build technologies in support of collaborative and participatory policymaking?
- How can we best share what we've learned and describe the barriers we face so as to inform and influence policymaking?
- How can you best inform us about community priorities and needs from other issues areas?
- How can we work together to adopt privacy and security priorities for all of our policies?

Funders

Questions for those in positions to fund social impact and technology to ask policymakers:

- How can our resources be combined with yours to accelerate or ensure participatory processes?
- What public–private partnerships could be established in service to the internet and technology development needs in our communities?
- How can we share what we've learned and tried with new models and efforts so as to support emerging policies?
- How can we surface and share successful stories from other regions or sectors in order to inform new policies?
- Are there potential gaps in available knowledge or data that we could resource for research and evaluation?

Policymakers

Questions for those creating and enforcing policies around technology and social impact to ask their peers:

- How do you verify and validate your information sources?
- How are you actively working to remove bias in your policymaking process?

- What participatory processes have been successful for you?
- How can we best share community priorities and needs from different policy topic areas?
- How are you reporting back on progress and challenges in policy-making initiatives?

Communities

Questions for community members to ask policymakers:

- How can we work together to change policies so as to increase funders' annual distributions?
- How might policy support new mechanisms for providing resources to our community?
- How can we work together to build policy protections for communities, individuals, and users?
- How can policies better force accountability among users and technology providers and social impact service providers?
- If any technology harms come from there being a lack of policy, are you prepared to be accountable for that?

Chapter Seven
Changing Conditions for Communities

In all of our discussions about social impact organizations, technology development, funding, and policymaking, we've stressed focusing on community connection, participation, and leadership. That focus must be reinforced by supporting community members in their efforts to engage and lead; they need resources to help them build skills, design solutions, direct funding, and decide on policies. And an essential aspect of that support calls for removing barriers to community access and participation in social impact work, technology development, resource allocation, and policymaking.

As we've said before, technology is constantly changing, which creates real challenges in training for and then maintaining the technological capacity within an organization. That challenge is made even harder by the fact that communities are made up of a widely diverse range of individuals who possess a widely diverse spread of experience, training, and confidence with technology. This complicates the need to upskill a community, and illustrates the importance of supporting parallel initiatives rather than relying on simplified solutions.

The work to change our world and to build what comes next will be inherently complicated. And when things get complicated, the most influential decision we make is to define what we value. As outlined in chapter 2, so many of the values for an equitable world are central to the understanding of community—from focusing on lived experience and accessibility to including a diversity of people and supporting a diversity of efforts to learn from. And so, directly central to a discussion of community is the power we have when we build our vision of what comes next together, with everyone's skills and expertise and brilliance brought to the table.

There are a multitude of questions that can guide us in building what comes next:

- What might community ownership look like?
- Who is making social change?
- How do we invest resources into the emergent and collaborative spaces where solutions could emerge?

We believe that the best way communities can pursue creating a better world will be to eliminate the barriers that prevent community leaders, community members, and communities from designing solutions that meet their needs—as well as to eliminate the barriers to being supported and funded in the ways social impact organizations and technology developers are privileged to be.

In chapters 3 and 4, we talked about technology in relation to social impact, both how it is put to use and how it can be better designed and developed. In chapters 5 and 6, we discussed the ways technology is funded and the way policies can support technology use and development. In this chapter, we highlight the shifts and investments necessary for creating conditions in which communities can lead.

CASE STUDY: ATUTU'S PROJECT SUNBIRD

Centering the community has been a constant refrain here—it is crucial that the community members who are affected by, benefit from, or otherwise participate in the programs or with the technologies are brought into the process. To follow is just one example of a successful community-centered approach.

Lin Thu Hein was born and raised in the northernmost state of Kachin in Myanmar until he moved to the United States when he was 13. Growing up in what he knows many consider a "developing country" influenced Lin's perception of what building solutions for or in communities can mean. Here he shares a prime example of how the best first step in trying to help others is to ask them what they need.

> Once a year, we would receive mosquito nets [from the United Nations]. . . .Most of us already had mosquito nets at home. We didn't need the ones they gave out, but my family took it in case we had guests. We didn't really like what they were giving out either. The mosquito nets they gave out were made from nylon or fiber materials that came out to be rigid and felt harsh against our skin. We preferred our nets to be made from cotton or softer materials, which were available in our markets. It was commonly understood in the community that the nets they gave out were also soaked in some sort of bug repellent, which ended up irritating our eyes and nose while using them. Things like this caused the community members to not adopt the nets the UN gave. And yet we got the same nets each year, so we just used them as spares or to catch fish in the monsoon season. If we felt mosquito nets were a priority, we would have bought them already or found a way to obtain one. We wouldn't really be waiting for the UN.

To Lin, this exemplifies the challenges with top-down solution design. "Coming to the US and going to college here to learn about engineering and development, I can see how those ideas come about. They come from good intentions, but the disconnect is in lack of community representation—and the assumptions we make as development practitioners can have harmful impacts on the community if they aren't part of the process."

As a student in humanitarian engineering, Lin experienced technology projects that employed a design-thinking approach, a model for development that prioritizes customer needs and rapid prototyping for testing, and quickly found that, although a step in the right direction, it still wasn't enough.

> You have to check your ego at the door and be humble. In the racial justice movement we learn to be allies, and in the development sector we similarly need to learn to be allies and not be the highlight of the room. That's difficult. You feel it when you show up to these communities—even though I speak fluent Burmese, when I show up [to help people in Myanmar] people see me as someone from California. That's the silent message in the room; we feel it: We have the ability to get on the plane or turn off the news and turn off our phones. We have the ability to look away from their pain. If we are going to do more needs assessment and ideation from a community-centered model, we need to remember that the communities were here long before us and will be here long after us. There's no need to ask "what problem are you facing?" because they have already addressed their problems.
>
> We as visitors to the community—people with power—don't need to solve their problems; we need to address what is blocking them from doing what they want. When I talk to young folks in Myanmar and ask, "What do you want to do? Let's dream!" I hear, "I want to be a musician. I want to be an electricity provider for my community. I want to be a teacher." And it is usually followed by, "But it'll probably never happen." That's a trigger for me that there's more to explore there, because that points to a systemic barrier that maybe we can address.

In 2017, Lin cofounded Atutu, a global design studio that partners with individuals and organizations around the world on social innovation initiatives that promote equitable and sustainable community development. Project Sunbird was Atutu's first endeavor. Initially they planned to develop and install solar-powered street lighting for communities in Myanmar. But fortunately they first got feedback from the community, and learned that indoor lighting was far more of a priority. This was the first moment of many where the ideas of the visiting team were revised by the community team—leading to superior outcomes. Based on that, it was determined that they would support the community in developing solar technology for indoor use. From the start, the team's programming and technology plans stemmed from a two-part vision: increasing equity and justice while also valuing community ownership and leadership.

When Lin and his team from University of California at San Diego engaged with local contacts in Kachin, a couple of important pieces of what is now Atutu's design model came into place. First, they formalized leadership in the community by identifying Atutu Fellows: the youth in the community who would be the primary participants—and the ones to whom ownership and maintenance would be turned over once the project was successful. Project Sunbird's Fellows included Hein Htet Aung, Tsaw Htoi, Mung Dan Aung, Myo Win Aung, Chit Oo Maung, Zaw Htoi Aung, Zaw Latt Aung, and Gum Lawt Aung. Second, in order to ensure the project could be operated independently, they decided to source the necessary parts and tools from Myanmar, not the United States. It wouldn't make sense for the visiting team to engineer a solution in California and mail it out to Myanmar for the Fellows to test; the Fellows needed to lead the design and the testing. But it also didn't feel right to build up their skills in a traditional capacity-building method. As Lin explains, this was where the concept of capacity matching emerged.

We've heard of the idea of capacity building: when we give tools and resources to a community and expect them to be self-sufficient with them. But when we started working with the

Fellows closely, we couldn't use that model because we didn't want to regiment their technology skills and outlook. We wanted to meet them where they were. We had an idea of where we needed the Fellows to be if we wanted them to be self-sufficient in providing lighting resources for their community, but we needed to focus on where they were. So we had many conversations with them about what they were already able to do. The Fellows didn't know how to work with micro controllers or high-end IOT [internet of things] technology because they had never really interacted with a computer before. We found out that the Fellows were really comfortable playing around with electricity—if they wanted something installed in their house, they would do it themselves. Some of them had worked as apprentices in car workshops and TV repair shops, so they knew how to work with wires and electricity and batteries. We started working on scaffolded learning, where we would take them just a little bit outside of their current capacity so they were challenged but not set up for failure—and slowly grow their capacity from there.

The capacity-matching approach meant that both the visiting team and the community team learned together. The visiting team started working with local materials the community team was already working with, including ceiling lights and batteries like those used in motorcycles and cars. Atutu committed to covering the costs for the pilot round of the first five light installations—after which their still jointly developed implementations would be locally funded.

The Fellows selected a remote school for the five pilot installations. The teachers there ran an after-school program for students who were falling behind in their studies. Since they had no electricity for indoor lighting, in the evenings they had to resort to candlelight in the teachers' dormitory. Access to solar lighting would transform their options for teaching and supporting students at the school. The community team and the visiting team each started to gather the various parts that were available to create and iterate to find what might work.

Lin shares how it proved a bit challenging for the visiting team to leverage their expertise and resources while still supporting the Fellows as the leaders.

> There were times where we got it wrong. For example, the charge controllers we used for the first five installations were locally sourced. When the visiting team tested them in California, they seemed fine, so we thought they would work. But when the Fellows installed them at the school, they said, "We are installing those in bedrooms, and they're loud. People can't sleep!" That was a result of our privilege, because we were doing lab testing by leaving it in the lab overnight, going back home and sleeping soundly, then only checking if it worked when we came back to the lab. Ultimately, they had to use it because it was all we had at the time, but we knew we couldn't keep using it. A few months later, once they had capital, they went back and swapped them out for a better option.

In selecting this site, the Fellows had wanted to aid a worthy cause while also demonstrating the possibility of solar lighting to the community; they hoped the project would build trust and interest—and generate requests for paid installations. Their plan worked. During the 18-month span of the Atutu project, the Fellows were hired to install solar lighting in about 80 homes.

Core to Atutu's approach is the goal of graduating projects when the need is met and it's clear the Fellows can sustain the work on their own. The Fellows demonstrated they were ready for this handoff in that they ordered all their own parts, provided all maintenance and repairs, and had sufficient interest in their services. Project Sunbird was considered complete when, roughly 18 months after they started, the Fellows received a contract to install solar lighting for a new community of 30 homes.

Lin remains committed to a community-driven model. He experienced firsthand how it's insufficient to try to help a community by hearing from them, learning from them—and providing solutions for them. The best results emerged when local community members were not only included in the endeavor but also positioned as the expert leaders, and then supported in that role.

"I am working more on seeing systemic barriers and historical oppression that the communities have experienced," Lin shares. "Instead of us being the experts or even trying to learn about all of what they know, I try to focus on how we can center their lived experience directly."

Community-centered change requires that resources, support, and training be invested toward the community's ability to lead, sustain, and own what will be the best solutions for them.

INSIDE THE PRACTICE OF CHANGE

Echoed in the story of Project Sunbird is a phrase that has come up many times in our work and organizing experiences: representation is not participation. Just because Lin was born and raised in Myanmar—and even had family members in the community where the project was rooted—did not mean that his representation on the team could account for the current lived experience, wisdom, knowledge, and realities of those living there today. Similarly, representing a community by hearing from them and learning from them does not equal their participation in the solution; even more so, as Lin noted, sharing an identity does not mean the current realities or priorities are automatically understood.

Unfortunately, so many of the dominant systems around us often reinforce or incentivize systemic exclusion wherein funding goes to those who already have access to it, visibility is limited to those who already are known, policies serve those who already have influence, and resources go to those already connected to funding institutions. In chapter 2, we said that the work to build what comes next would require us to make changes in ourselves, our organizations, and our world. That change for systemic inclusion starts with letting go of a few things. The systems and expectations of exclusion that say only certain people or institutions are worthy of funding don't serve us in truly building relationships and collaborating. The myths and stereotypes that tell us only certain organizations can make change, or that only those with certain degrees can lead, shut out many alternatives. And the idea that companies should have more power than communities benefits only the companies.

Fortunately, we have the option to let those things go. We have the option to change. How might we begin?

Changing Structures and Systems

Some of the most challenging dynamics for communities to work through are practices and policies that can feel bigger than any group of individuals. The regulations that dictate and perpetuate problematic limitations in philanthropic grantmaking, technology development funding, and private ownership inhibit innovation, accelerated impact, and widespread collaboration. Changing those systems will take concerted work by an especially broad coalition of stakeholders, but it can be done. The first step will be finding ways to build tolerance for change and trust outside of the current limits.

Move Beyond Charity Designations   Who's making change today? Is change the exclusive domain of designated 501(c)(3) nonprofit organizations in the States, registered charities in Canada, and other nongovernmental organizations around the world? Quite certainly not. Many different kinds of passionate organizations, groups, and leaders are dedicated to taking on the work to provide services and support communities. Let's celebrate that fact and bolster their efforts.

Consider how different, for example, the pandemic response-and-relief efforts could have looked if some of the primary mutual aid and grassroots efforts had been eligible for funding, grants, training, and technology products to more efficiently facilitate their efforts. In the face of pandemic-related shutdowns, income drops, and more, many regional and geographic communities across the States and around the world found strength in community, as highlighted in creative, resourceful responses to COVID. Community members shared and received everything from clean socks and coats to fresh meals and storable foods. Neighbors offered what they could and others took what they needed, many sharing stories of giving and receiving under different trying circumstances. Had networks or community leaders qualified for funding from local grantmakers or government grant programs, consistently stocked pantries and fridges would have eased hunger and provided a sense of stability in uncertain times in more locations and through more means than exclusively relying on established nonprofit food banks. As we discussed in chapter 5, philanthropy is not the only sector overly reliant on the status of registered nonprofits or charities as a qualification for support; so too do technology providers restrict affordable options to those with a government-issued nonprofit status. If those same community leaders supporting free pantries had qualified for more sophisticated technologies, they could have more easily coordinated the hosts and owners of the fridges and pantries across the city, organized more events for community builds and repairs, and provided communications and updates across subscribers' preferred channels.

The rigid belief that only recognized groups can be trusted to lead such work, and manage the resources to do that work, stunts the abilities of communities willing to contribute while denying all of us the benefit of additional parties working to fill the gaps. It also denies resources to a social impact sector that is already operating under strained capacity. This rigid belief is held by funders requiring that recipients be registered nonprofits, as well as by technology providers who use that same designation to limit who qualifies for free or discounted software.

Chris Worman cofounded Connect Humanity[1], an organization building a community of practice and investment vehicles dedicated to supporting, catalyzing, and scaling solutions that address barriers to internet access. Chris has observed this same paradox:

> Who has access to what technology—at least the donated or discounted technology made available through CSR programming—has been largely determined by whether or not the recipient is a legal entity. That model assumes [that] any other kind of entity would not do good with the tech; that all organizations can get registered (not true in some countries); and that nonprofit corporations are the best way to do social good (arguable). The result is a narrow view of civil society and severe limits on the socially beneficial usage of technologies. At best, this is rather contrary to the stated purposes of the programs making these products or services available in the first place. At worst, it leads to terms like "digital apartheid" being whispered. We are smart enough to do better. There is little reason that, in this age of information and cloud-based tech, we can't build new models that start from a position of trusting the intent of a user.

Some may say that only certain groups can be trusted with resources—financial or technological—because the nature of their certification and reporting requirements creates protections that guarantee those investments are best and properly used. This simply isn't true, or it doesn't have to be. There's no reason that grassroots efforts, groups that intentionally organize outside of the certified nonprofit entity structure, and mutual aid efforts can't be expected to use funds or technology donations as effectively and accountably as those that are registered organizations. Add to which, many mutual aid efforts and grassroots campaigns regularly make transparent the donations received and the receipts for intended purchases, even providing full accounting to the community about where resources are invested. To doubt the reliability, efficacy, and integrity of community groups is a complete denial of the concept that people are capable of organizing and creating value outside of a corporate structure. The power of being in relationship as community members, as coalitions, and as leaders is central to the work to change our world.

Resource Communities Holistically   A recurring refrain throughout this book has been the invitation to open our imaginations to think about doing everything—from social impact work to technology development to funding to policymaking—differently. Central to the idea of imagining new ways of working together is the challenge to be open to changing process or investment without necessarily being completely assured of the outcome, or even having defined the results. If we want to improve any and every corner of the systems and structures we have today, the challenge is for us to support and encourage change without expecting to know exactly how that change may happen or how it will work out.

To bring communities into leadership, and to harness collective support in service to that leadership, those communities must be provided resources—including technology tools, money, infrastructure, access, training, and more—without restrictions regarding who gets to take part in the mission. This requires trust that the community knows best what is needed—just as we saw demonstrated by Project Sunbird.

Angela Siefer is the Executive Director of the National Digital Inclusion Alliance, a community of digital inclusion practitioners and advocates. She sees many sectors carrying a responsibility to ensure that communities can lead and are supported doing so. She shares, "Helping community members learn to be advocates is something that a lot of us have a responsibility to do. Organizations should take on that responsibility. Funders should take on that responsibility. If we don't [address this], then the imbalance we have will continue."

Bringing together a diversity of resources for community support is also necessary for changing how policies are made and who gets to make them. "We've been intentionally led to believe that there is a distinction between policy and our individual lives, but that's a myth," explains Vanice Dunn, Vice President of Communications at PolicyLink, a national research and action institute advancing racial and economic equity.[2] "Every decision, opportunity, or barrier we encounter every day is the result of a policy, either past or present. We have to break down the false wall and make clear to both policymakers and our communities at large that policy is the force that drives our experiences, and we have the power to shape policy in a way that betters our lives and paves the way for a new future."

Technology development is not exempt from this conversation either. Dr. Fallon Wilson is the Co-Founder of #BlackTechFutures Research Institute, which works to grow a National Black Tech Ecosystem through research, #blacktechpolicy, and data-driven intervention. She says that social impact organizations and technology developers should "always first build relationships and trust with the people their technology is supposed to help. Then, share the profits from their social impact work with the people their technology is supposed to help."[3]

A holistic approach necessarily considers not just the conditions and resources necessary for change, but also who will share the benefits. What might it look like to establish community-based centers for training and building technology, for changemaking and policymaking that are localized and community led? As Fallon says, "Fund Black dreams in this space!" What if we change our mindset? Instead of integrating and incorporating community feedback in projects that meet the goals of our organizations, what if we devote the resources we have across these sectors to fulfill the dreams of the community?

Build Intentional Accountability   In chapter 2, we said that the world we want is one where technology is accountable to communities. As Fallon suggested, one element of creating accountability calls for being in relationship with the communities that our technologies and social impact programs serve. Another element of the necessary trust- and relationship-building processes calls for committing to interoperability.

Interoperability is the concept that if something new is developed, it should be able to work with existing options. For us, this idea contends that if a service were required to work regardless of the kind of device used to access it, or if a user's data and content were easily exported and transported elsewhere at any time, then programs, services, and technologies would be much better developed toward user needs—and thus by design (more) accountable to users. This is an important concept for many to consider, from technology developers to social impact organizations to policymakers and funders.

As we shift the ways social impact work is done and by whom, we can intentionally build in accountability with commitments and standards that require interoperability for the participant—regardless of the type of organization they engage with or the kinds of services they receive. Similarly, as we change technology development projects and processes to include community members throughout, we can add accountability by enforcing expectations and policy for interoperability that protects a user's data and content—honoring it as theirs to keep, move, reuse, or share on their own terms.

In adding these accountabilities, we must acknowledge that some technologies cause harm: from built-in bias like facial recognition tools to inappropriate data sets and analysis that profile or exclude communities and individuals because of their identities or past actions. Not every technology needs to be used for social impact work, and not every technology we have today will come with us as we build a better world together. There is value in bringing together ethical experts and communities who have experienced these harms to work together on what expectations for interoperability can be, and to collectively be the ones to set those expectations for policymakers and organizations to move forward into standards and policies.

Enabling Communities

Before social impact organizations can expect community members to do various things online—such as manage their own data and access programs or benefits—those communities need to be able to get online. Before technology teams can expect community members to fully engage in development projects, those communities need to be invested in training and skill building. Before we put policies and parameters around access to the best tools for organizing and advocating for change, communities need to be supported in understanding and navigating these spaces. When historical and current barriers keep communities and community members out of change-making, out of managing their own services, and out of the spaces where potential solutions are designed, better outcomes aren't possible. Enabling communities requires investing in the foundations of their success.

Ubiquitous Access Is Necessary   First things first: without reliable and affordable internet access available in every neighborhood and from every home, we cannot invite or expect community members to be part of social impact organizations' work or be involved in developing technologies—or even to be able to advocate fully for their priorities. It is time for internet access to be understood and provided as the public utility it is.

BroadbandNow, which publishes independent research on broadband in the United States, has surfaced discrepancies and issues with the way access is reported by the Federal Communications Commission (FCC):[4]

> The FCC's 2019 Broadband Deployment Report stated that 21.3 million Americans lack access to broadband internet, including wired and fixed wireless connections. In its 2020 report, the FCC claimed that the number of Americans without access to broadband fell to 14.5 million.
>
> The figures and estimates cited by the FCC rely upon semi-annual self-reporting by internet service providers (ISPs) using the FCC-mandated "Form 477." However, there is a widely acknowledged flaw with Form 477 reporting: if an ISP offers service to at least one household in a census block, then the FCC counts the entire census block as covered by that provider.

We can immediately see the issue with this manner of reporting on service availability. BroadbandNow investigated to find a more accurate scale of service provision in the United States:

> [In 2020], we manually checked availability of more than 11,000 addresses using Federal Communications Commission (FCC) Form 477 data as the "source of truth." Based on the results, we estimated that 42 million Americans do not have the ability to purchase broadband internet.
>
> In 2021, we expanded our study, manually checking availability of terrestrial broadband internet (wired or fixed wireless) for more than 58,000 addresses. In all, we checked more than 110,000 address-provider combinations using the FCC Form 477 data as the "source of truth."
>
> This study confirms our estimate that at least 42 million Americans do not have access to broadband.

This figure that BroadbandNow surfaced doesn't include the full extent of how many are offline. That real total includes people who have access but don't have the skills and devices to make purchasing it relevant, as well as people who live in areas where service is available but not affordable. And, of course, this only considers internet exclusion in the United States.

Looking at the global context, Chris Worman explains:

> In addition to more, and more appropriate, support for everything that comes after one has connected to the internet, there is a pressing need to increase investment in accelerating the rate at which the world's 3.5 billion unconnected people come online. Telecoms and governments have not, and will not, connect the world. That work is being done by nontraditional, often community-owned operators. Nontraditional operators consistently provide the fastest, cheapest internet on the planet while putting the power and profit of the internet back in the hands of those who would otherwise remain unconnected. Yet they are wildly underfunded. They need philanthropic support for community organizing, advocacy, and planning grants. They need low-interest loans to begin building out their networks that, almost inevitably, become self-sustaining. They need a blend of type and size of finance, organized to meet their needs.
>
> Options for increasing the amount of funds available could come simply from increased allocation from governments, spectrum sales, bonds, or the release of latent capital—such as frozen kleptocratic assets or the reinvestment of Foreign Corrupt Practice Act fines—back into local, democracy-enabling, digital infrastructures. Increased funds could in some cases be deployed through existing government funding vehicles dedicated to digital policy, skills and literacy, and civic tech. A new partnership and funding vehicle will likely be needed for regulatory and governance technologies considering the necessity to partner directly with government agencies on regulatory tech, and considering that many governance technologies might be best deployed at scale in partnership with the standard operating technologies used by governments. New partnerships able to

most effectively channel government support could be built in partnership with private philanthropy through the establishment of Trusts for Digital Democracies similar to the partnerships that led to the democracy trusts across Central and Eastern Europe.

This problem won't be solved by simply waiting for corporate internet providers to build networks for currently unserved or under-served communities, especially those that have not been consistently and historically prioritized—including tribal communities and both rural and geographically disconnected areas. As Chris notes, public–private partnerships and government funding can increase rollout to new areas. And, as Karl Bode reported for *Motherboard* in September 2021, "More than a thousand US communities have now built their own broadband networks."[5] Communities building their own solutions is not new, and it's not new for broadband either. But the acceler-ated rate at which communities are launching their own broadband initiatives demonstrates the clear need for connectivity and the value of replicating successful projects in new areas. There is no single model in use; a number of models have been successful in various communities, as well as successfully shared with other communities, as Karl reports:

> The Institute for Local Self-Reliance (ILSR) maintains a data-base and interactive map tracking community owned and oper-ated broadband networks. Such networks take many forms, whether it's a broadband network built on the back of a local power utility, a local government-run ISP built from scratch, or a locally-owned cooperative.
>
> ILSR told Motherboard that its latest data shows that 83 municipal networks now deliver publicly owned fiber across 148 communities, up from 63 such networks early last year. Fifty-seven communities now operate their own cable broad-band network, 600 networks are built on the back of local gov-ernments, and hundreds more are regional cooperatives.

Local networks are partly about local ownership, and, importantly, also part of achieving the kind of localization and customization for community needs that other types of community-centered technology development should include. MuralNet is a nonprofit organization addressing digital divides by bringing the internet to homes on tribal lands; they partner "with government agencies, Silicon Valley, middle-mile providers, ISPs, colleges and universities to provide Tribes with access to equipment and in-house network planning, labor, technical support, policy specialists and lawyers."[6] MuralNet's support to tribal communities to deploy local networks is not simply about replicating the same approach and solutions, but truly focuses on local sustainability including leadership and ownership for the projects, including the Community Builds program, which is "a working group-centered incubator focused on building the internal capacity of Tribes to design, deploy, maintain and grow their own sustainable community networks. Through experimentation and refinement, participating Tribal communities are already providing valuable feedback, key learnings and reference architecture to accelerate deployments and help develop trainings for sustainable wireless networks for all Tribal communities across the United States."[7]

Ultimately, an equitable world requires ubiquitous, affordable, reliable access to the internet, and this access is a prerequisite for communities to be able to efficiently and consistently engage with social impact organizations, technology development, and policymaking.

The Tech Pipeline Is a Continuum   Over the last 20 years (and beyond), significant investment in Science, Technology, Engineering, and Math (STEM) education has focused on youth, especially those in K–12, with the hope of sparking passions and interest in these areas—and propelling them into university and training programs, then eventually into STEM-related professional fields. But, as it happens, getting more people into these programs and fields isn't the only potential benefit of focusing on STEM education; the reality is that knowledge, skills, and confidence with STEM topics is something that equips every person to engage fully in a digital world.

As technology continues to evolve, all of us need to be invested in the "tech pipeline" actually being a continuum of learning for everyone. When we adopt that perspective, at least to some degree, the way we make that knowledge accessible naturally changes. Learning about technology and tech development, learning about engineering and data, even learning about problem solving can't be limited to academic institutions—especially privileged institutions that already struggle with equity issues.

Reframing training and learning as a continuum can help us connect what are currently siloed areas of skill building—from the on-the-job training for employees across sectors to after-school programs for teens to fellowships with in-the-field placements to apprenticeships. Committing to a continuum approach pulls together social impact organizations, technologists, funders, and policymakers to better integrate and design support systems that more effectively and accessibly support more communities using technology and building technology— and ultimately changing the world.

New Models for Change

We know that building an equitable world will require new models of social impact work, technology development, funding, and policymaking. But what are the new models ahead for communities? There will not be one answer; we know that much. There is not—there cannot be—one option for everything, because localized difference is necessary and beautiful. When replicating in one community a project, program, or software that worked in another, adjusting to local norms or goals or structures is the key to making it work. Fortunately, communities are both good adopters and good adapters when their needs are prioritized, as Project Sunbird demonstrated.

Lyel Resner is Visiting Lecturer and Head of Public Interest Technology Studio at Cornell Tech. He explains: "If you're impact first, you should develop the infrastructure, orientation, and capability to make cross-sector investments. None of the problems we're facing can be solved in one sector. Invest in all vehicles—501(c)(4) to 501(c)(3) to Public Benefit Corporation to S Corporations."[8] The ways we resource for new models require us to consider as many different kinds of participants as possible, including organization and registered entity type, experience levels, community sizes, and even collaborations and partnerships.

And if we are ready to embrace a reality where what we need next and what comes next calls on our imagination, we need to ask how we can shift our thinking and our collaboration into models that allow for emergent solutions, open-ended learning, and diverse relationships. Said another way, we need to invest in social infrastructure without expecting to have the regular partners at the table signing nondisclosure agreements and committing to a predetermined scope of work. What could we create together without requiring that we know from the beginning what the end point will be?

"I've been fortunate to see several ways people who get things done are nurtured, and how their connections with each other are fostered," says Sabrina Roach, a digital equity practitioner and advocate.[9] "I've seen how sometimes it is a value just to bring those people together to build social infrastructure. They may do projects together way down the line that are bigger and have a more amplified impact," but what that impact ends up being and what those projects are that contributed to it weren't anticipated or defined when they started collaborating. The investment was for them as community members and leaders to have space and connection with each other to think and dream. "What kinds of relationship infrastructure have been built during this time of crisis that will pay off in community-led projects down the line?" Sabrina asks. We know that funding has been critical for so many immediate needs across communities and social impact organizations; but has there also been funding and resourcing for the open-ended social infrastructure to build better futures with?

Social infrastructure is not, of course, just for community leaders and members; it is needed with and among social impact organizations, technology developers, funders, and policymakers as well. Indeed, it is needed among all those five groups. Emergent solutions can be seen and explored when we collectively invest in creating the space in and from which community leaders can emerge and be enlisted to participate in the social infrastructure. Sabrina sees social infrastructure as a flexible concept that could be achieved in many ways: "Invest in connective tissue for communities. Fund convenings, collaborations, partnerships, coalitions. Essentially, fund support staff for the community. Nationally, regionally, locally."

Sabrina sees resources for educating, encouraging, inspiring, and communicating with and between these groups in programs and technology that many overlook. "We are leaving neighborhood-level social infrastructure, trust, resources, and richness on the table when we leave out public access education and government television, low-power FM and community radio. We are leaving out these actual, physical, in-community anchor points." Why are we overlooking these resources? Is it because we are, again, caught prioritizing only new technologies and new programs? When we do that we lessen our ability to make change. There are many things we could learn from those who helped invest and spur the rollout of these community anchor points decades ago. Using that learning in new ways today, and maybe even using the systems and technologies available through those programs, may be an important part of how we build what comes next.

Whether it is previously successful models applied in new sectors or tested technology customized for new use, the work to invest in the infrastructure that supports us is critical to the foundation of how we engage with each other in the process of working to build a new world.

Sam Chenkin, a nonprofit organizer and activist, understands how needed this is:[10]

> I'm not sure the answers to participatory technology creation are really unique or new or have anything to do with the field of technology. It seems to me that we'll build more equitable and transformative tools as a natural result of building more equitable and transformative institutions and communities. We don't need a formal framework—we need relationships with our community. We don't need participatory design—we need those facing systemic oppression to be the ones in charge. Organizations and systems that are accountable and effective are a precondition to building technologies that are accountable and effective. Technology is just another tool in the larger movement for liberation.

In the end, what we need is each other. Relationships enable accountability, failures and tests enable learning, investment and support enable trust and opportunity.

QUESTIONS FOR WHAT'S NEXT

Changemaking should not be constrained to organizations of a certain kind; truly there is a vast amount of opportunity for improving our world and it will take everyone contributing to make it happen. The ways social impact and community resourcing are viewed need to broaden to include those operating and organizing outside of registered entities, include coalitions and networks, and embrace that there is value in investing in leaders and relationships even without a specific project plan in front of them.

Together, across all the groups discussed in these last five chapters, we need to share more of what we learn, test, and build together, and be more committed to advancing ideas as we learn instead of always seeking something brand-new. We need to release the false binary view that new is good and not-new is bad, or at least is boring. Replication is not inherently bad, especially when we can work together to customize our social services, technology tools, and collaborative models to meet shared needs and preferences as a community. The following questions are designed to support community members moving these ideas into conversation with others so that, together, our momentum can build toward change.

Social Impact Organizations

Questions for those working in and with social impact efforts to ask the communities they work with:

- Do you have positive or negative examples of working with a social impact organization? If so, what are they?
- Who in your community are the key decision makers who must be brought along with any change?
- Are there decision-making or planning norms and expectations that we can honor and follow?
- What privileges, power, or access can be extended in service to your priorities?
- What are your biggest priorities within our mission?

Technologists

Questions for those building technology for social impact to ask communities their technologies benefit or affect:

- What level of tech literacy/proficiency does your community have? What would you like it to be?
- What support or resources would you need to have to view participating in the development process as useful?
- In what ways has this community been harmed or negatively affected by technology?

- Who would be harmed if the technology we build fails?
- Who will profit and benefit the most from the technology we build?

Funders

Questions for those in positions to fund social impact and technology to ask of the communities impacted or involved:

- We believe that we could enable funding outside of established organizational structures if we established trust. How can we do that?
- How can we collaborate on new models of ownership for technologies developed in the community with our funding?
- How will you tell the story of this work or project to share what you learn with others?
- How have you already tried or tested this project? What other projects are ready for investment?
- What expectations should we set for return on investment?

Policymakers

Questions for those creating and enforcing policies around technology and social impact to ask communities impacted or benefited:

- What technologies or services do you not currently have access to, either because of availability or affordability?
- What experiences or knowledge do you have that you could share with us for better policymaking?
- It's important to us that we stay in communication with you and your community in a manner that honors individuals' needs and time commitments and is accessible to all. How can we best do that?
- How can we best elevate your voices and stories in the policymaking process without being extractive?

- What can we do to support community access and participation in policymaking?

Communities

Questions for community members to ask each other:

- How did you get started?
- What have you tried? What have you learned? What's worth repeating or reusing?
- In pushing for change, technology development, or other investment, how did you decide what work to take on and what not to take on?
- What are our dreams?
- What resources do we already have that we can use?

Chapter Eight
Start Building Power for What's Next

Now that we have examined the roles of key players in the social impact ecosystem and explored how to expand access, it is time to consider how the work to build the tech that comes next might actually be done.

The Social Impact Organizations That Come Next

We have already discussed how important it is to consider not just what work social impact organizations do but also *how* they do the work they perform. By involving all staff in strategic conversations about technology, social impact organizations can adopt and increase an organizational culture that keeps the focus on the mission and community instead of on the technical tools, allowing for investments in technology to be more successful. The implemented technology should help with repetitive, straightforward tasks that people shouldn't have to spend their time on, thereby freeing them to work on the many activities that require a human's attention, empathy, and judgment. While changing individual mindsets about technology is important, the impact can be magnified if organizations move away from a scarcity mindset and act on the value of collaboration within the sector; leveraging shared infrastructure can allow organizations to more quickly launch and sunset programs, as well as test and learn from the work they do.

The Technologists That Come Next

Technologists in the social impact sector serve a broad variety of functions. Whether a technical designer, developer, or implementer of a tool or program, technologists must have deep subject matter expertise. They must understand when to implement complex algorithms and structures and when to mitigate harms—as well as when to acknowledge that the solution needed is not a technical one. Furthermore, social impact technologists must invest the time to connect with organizations and communities in the space to understand true needs. To strengthen the ties to the community, technologists must be able to include non-technologists in decision making and plainly explain how the data and tech are used. For technologists to develop technology differently, they must build upon a foundation of security, privacy, and ethical use as they bring nontechnologists along in the development process.

The Funders That Come Next

How money is injected, managed, and used in the social impact sector matters. Funders—whether philanthropists, venture capitalists, or business owners—can fund thoughtful, inclusive development and implementation of technology. Structures can be put in place to give the organizations themselves the space to innovate, the freedom to learn from activities that didn't work the first time, and the flexibility to create based on what the organizations, as the on-the-ground actors, know to be true based on their experiences. Formal communication loops can be built to allow community members to have some agency over decisions directly affecting their lives. Funders must seek ways to ensure proximity to impact. By funding social impact organizations to hire or work closely with developers, the technology solutions are situated in direct relationship to the issues and regions being addressed. This also creates a foundation for iteration and evolution of the technologies in context, where development staff can make changes and improvements as real-world use cases present new opportunities.

The Policymakers That Come Next

Policymakers, we have learned, have the ability to restructure policymaking to involve more people in the process and to incorporate technical expertise into the process. Although there will likely never be policymakers who have expertise in the policy, technology, and other issues facing all social impact organizations, we can expand pathways for technologists and the organizations to articulate their policy needs and influence the policymaking process. It will continue to be important for social impact organizations to build coalitions to engage in policymaking. And because it would be untenable to leave key policy decisions to individual technologists who don't have a holistic view across applications and implications, a subset of technologists must be willing to work alongside policymakers to bring needed oversight to the technical development process.

The Community That Comes Next

Solutions that benefit the community can only do so if the community is an active participant in the development, testing, and deployment of these solutions. We must create structures and systems to allow communities to use their own power. This means ensuring communities are resourced holistically—that is, to consider what funding and technical support communities need to support their dreams. Shifting the perception that technology is only accessible by a handful of experts can also be beneficial to communities. Remember that expertise can be learned through traditional educational institutions, but it can also come from apprenticeships or other hands-on experiences. The organizations that support communities can take many different forms, and as we build for what comes next we should focus first on what we accomplish then create the structure—a 501(c)(3), a Public Benefit Corporation, or some yet to be defined construct—that will work best to deliver for the community.

START BUILDING POWER WHERE YOU ARE

Most organizations and individuals working in or around the social impact sector do not function today as we have described in previous chapters. Some organizations and individuals may be compelled by the vision presented in this book but lack clarity on how to start the transformation within their sphere of influence. Now that we've discussed how to drive change from these different perspectives, we can shift to discussing the tech that comes next from wherever you are in your journey.

Individuals and organizations can hold multiple roles—and often do. Social organizations, for example, can become funders if they are tasked with distributing money to other organizations or individuals. Funders can be technologists if they directly provide technical support to organizations. And technology organizations can be social impact organizations if they structure themselves as 501(c)(3) or other community-focused organizations. It is important, then, to recognize what role you and your organization are playing in each situation and to acknowledge where you need to grow and change.

Resistance Is Part of the Process

There are many, many inspirational quotes available on mugs, posters, and memes about being the change you want to see in the world, or how change is inevitable, or how change is necessary for growth. Maybe those encouragements are out there because change is difficult for many people. Change is even more difficult for organizations, let alone entire sectors. Therefore, as you begin, it's important to recognize some of the barriers that might present themselves. By holding to the values laid out in chapter 2—especially honoring lived experiences and being accountable to communities—you can begin to push back against any resistance you encounter. You might even recognize that the individuals expressing resistance may not be the ideal partners for your work.

Speed of impact. One common criticism you may get concerns how quickly changes occur. Technologists may be used to building fast and breaking things, and funders may want a quick return on investment so as to claim success. As we've discussed, however, building the process for inclusive design takes time; it's essential that everyone involved or affected feel they've had the opportunity to express their views. Of course, it would be impossible for everyone's vision to be specifically designed around, but many will appreciate that at least their preference was taken into consideration.

Sharing information. Dara Byrne, of the John Jay College example in chapter 4, indicated that after the partnership with DataKind they "stopped using the 'sage on a stage' model for sharing information" internally and externally. Traditional ways of working incentivize policymakers, technologists, and social impact organizations to hold and control knowledge and, therefore, power. In contrast, to build the tech that comes next, it's wise to reinforce that sharing information is a way to bring individuals and organizations along on the change journey, as well as a way to increase the likelihood that the developed and implemented technology will be relevant.

Apathy. Individuals in all roles might argue that they can't be expected to know everything, or that the current ways of operating are fine. Policymakers may feel the number of touchpoints that technology requires is so vast that it's hard to know where to start. Social impact organizations may have already invested in creating the level at which they currently function; they might resist spending time thinking about how things could be done differently, or they might doubt that different practices could yield better outcomes. However, Brandon Forester, National Organizer for Internet Rights and Platform Accountability at MediaJustice, warns against this sort of complacency: "People have to take the time to step back and think: 'Are the policies we are advocating for getting us closer to the liberated future we want, or are they half measures that in the long run will set us back?'"[1] Reinforcing the benefits of the ultimate impact you want to have, contrasted with the frustrations of the current state, may help in combating this type of resistance.

Stages of progress. Technologists, and occasionally funders, may suggest that building tech is a single-phase process—that once a new tool has been developed it won't need additional development. But as Robert Lee of Rescuing Leftover Cuisine (chapter 5) learned, "We know our website will never be 'finished.' We're constantly making improvements and building new functionality with a focus on creating a smooth, streamlined, and engaging experience for our rescuers." One way to counter the single-phase argument would be to point to examples of similar social impact organizations that built multiple versions of technology tools.

Bigger is better. Another type of resistance that funders and especially technologists may present is to push large solutions that worked in one environment into other environments, without analyzing the appropriateness or evaluating whether the needs—not only the technical systems—match. This often happens by assuming that large business solutions for tech and funding structures will work for any organization, regardless of size, or by assuming success is defined only by scale. "We have more experience with big technology decisions and investments than you do," may be something you hear. Push back on the temptation to act as though bigger is always better by highlighting your specific requirements and community.

As the suggestions following the types of resistance outlined here indicate, it is possible to build productive relationships to develop technology that serves and empowers communities, even with those who at first express dissent or reluctance. But we still consider it a red flag if a potential partner voices concerns like these. When individuals hold to their sentiments, or seem unwilling to be swayed, their reluctance can prevent collaboration. Ideally, all parties will be willing to engage in honest, open discussion, and any concerns will be worked through, proving that productive collaboration is possible.

Structuring People and Communities

The world we envision, as shown in the illustration of systemic inclusion in chapter 2, centers on the communities in which we live. It centers on people, with all their strengths and idiosyncrasies. Working with communities calls for helping community members feel valued so that they can make meaningful contributions to the mission. As many of us know, working with people can be, at various times, invigorating, disappointing, and challenging. Fortunately, organizing community members well is a skill that can be learned.

Dr. Michelle Montgomery Thompson, the Coordinator of WhoData.org, a New Orleans–based community-municipal-university partnership that uses an applied public participation geographic information system (PPGIS) model, teaches students to embed themselves into communities to help elicit critical data about the wealth communities truly have—as opposed to what traditional indicators show.[2] The projects ranged from property condition surveys to economic impact analyses of first-time homebuyer projects, using HUD-funded homes on formerly blighted parcels.

> Students would observe how to engage with community partners through a meeting in which the partner, such as Associate Neighborhood Development (AND), wanted to document the conditions of Hoffman Triangle. The residents wanted to have a

way to document and summarize illegal dumping, blighted properties, and city-owned lots that needed maintenance. AND wanted to identify potential first-time homebuyer development sites using Housing & Urban Development (HUD) soft-second mortgage programs. The City of New Orleans was interested in learning if and/or how neighborhood data could be used to complement information that was collected through the building department, planning commission, and other disparate offices.

By using the WhoData standardized field survey training guide, students and residents conducted "paper and pen" surveys to evaluate over 3,000 parcels in Hoffman Triangle. A student data team converted the paper surveys into Excel spreadsheets which were coded and translated into a spatial data format. The data was transformed into summary tables and maps, which were presented back to the community and shared with the City of New Orleans and local funders. Students were able to understand the complexity of working first-hand with community partners and how to go beyond what was initially expected for a community-university project within eight weeks.

Use of the GIS technology was crucial for transforming the data. The ability to have local knowledge and compare that with the public data (e.g. property ownership) increased the capacity of the project. Students were able to conduct data quality testing during the project, which increased its utility and validity. The work the students completed supported community participants in how to make more informed decisions with their money for themselves and their families.[3]

First, it is important to understand who composes the community. To build the technology that will serve communities and create an interconnected, inclusive world, we need to have better collaboration between social impact leaders, funders, technologists, and policymakers.

It's important to note that, although we have identified these four categories, other professions either fit into these categories or complement the work being done. Artists and storytellers, doctors and researchers—these are all necessary to create the community.

Second, social impact leaders should confidently name the community they serve. An inclusive world requires us to recognize unique differences and intentionally create solutions that serve historically overlooked communities. The work of what comes next is about justice and empowerment, and this can only be achieved if it is clear what is being remedied and what is being supported. The #BlackTechFutures Research Institute, for example, explicitly states that they are building "a national network of city-based researchers and practitioners conducting research on sustainable local black tech ecosystems."[4] Dr. Fallon Wilson, founder of #BlackTechFutures, sums up the need for this focus by saying, "So, often when we do this work of public interest technology we do it from the lens of how can 'I' make sure systematically discriminated communities are not once again violated by my work, instead of taking the time to build relationships with black and brown people to help co-design the work that we purport will be done for 'their' communities."[5] We must focus on relationship building and centering the community, rather than on how an external changemaker may make a difference. Clearly naming the situation allows all roles to orient themselves around the specific problems that need to be addressed.

STRUCTURE ORGANIZATIONS TO SUPPORT NEW MODELS

The systems and structures within an organization—whether the organization is for social impact, technology, or even funding—can greatly affect its ability to implement the changes discussed in this book. And so, to follow we explore how to make intentional shifts in the way organizations grow and hire technical talent.

Shift the Ways Employees Use Tech Internally

As we've said, a social sector organization can greatly advance their mission by using technology *differently*. This can begin by changing employees' relationship with technology. Different individuals can vary widely in their enthusiasm for new tech, or even their enthusiasm for any tech. As social impact organizations begin to adopt new technology—a new communication system, a new tool that tracks donors and volunteers, a new dashboard that analyzes operations—we can help shift the culture by formalizing the adoption of and engagement with technology. This could mean adding to employees' job descriptions that certain positions require interacting with the technology needed for the role. In addition, organizations can consider how best to document and communicate the need for employees to contribute to the development of new processes—and, when relevant, new technology for the organization.

Similarly, the use of technology should be seen as a strategic necessity. As organizations create strategic plans, write grant proposals, or communicate how they work, they should ensure that thoughtful use of technology is always articulated. Discussing technology alongside strategy, mission, and impact will also support the culture change that helps dissenters realize that technology adoption and mission execution are not in opposition, but that they actually work together to propel stronger organizations.

Hire to Support Community-driven Technology Solutions

Many social impact organizations may want to hire a full technical team but lack the budget for it. How, then, can organizations advance their strategic vision—including technology to advance the mission—with limited finances?

For organizations that do not have the funding for even one technical position, employing volunteer technologists is an option. Dr. Quincy Brown, a cofounder of blackcomputeHER.org, an influential think tank for Black women and girls in computing and tech, points out: "There are many technologists who can and will support social impact organizations as volunteers. Not just from the user side, but also from the design and implementation and research side."[6] It is important to note, however, that the criteria for partnering with volunteer technical talent are the same as hiring for staff technical talent: seek out individuals who have demonstrated technical expertise, as well as the ability and willingness to learn from and share with organizations and communities—who themselves have the systems to deliver on a schedule. In addition, the time to onboard a volunteer into an organization is often not trivial; when possible, it's wise to seek financial support to cover the time investment required for managing volunteer technical support.

Once funding has been secured to support in-house technical talent, the next question is which technologist position should be an organization's first hire. The key attributes of a social impact technologist are a deep understanding of the variety and limitations of technology, the humility to learn from the community, and the ability to execute. And so we recommend that the first hire be a director of technology. Essentially, this individual will need to

- make decisions on when to buy versus build versus collaborate with other entities on software;
- have a demonstrated ability to connect with the community and explain the hard tech in easy-to-understand ways;
- write and test code, as they will be the first line of defense of the organization's tech systems; and
- make decisions on when to seek support for user research, user design, and software engineering, as well as how to assess candidates for this support.

The decision of a second technical hire will depend on the specific needs of the organization and the relevant strategic goals. For larger organizations that already enjoy a large technical team, periodic reviews of the social impact organization's strategy, how it makes an impact in its mission area, and any policy or funding goals should be performed to make sure technology continues to advance the organization's mission, not compete with it. Regardless of the organization's size, remember that your organization is not the first to have to navigate tough choices about technology staffing. It is possible to figure it out, and you can build the support you need in your organization.

GET STARTED

Ultimately, only so much time can be spent studying the challenges in and of the social impact space. "Social problems have interest too," says Lyel Resner, technologist, entrepreneur, educator, and adviser. "They grow. They compound."[7] Whether you are a funder who can make capital available more quickly, a technologist who can expand the capabilities of mission-driven organizations, a social impact leader who knows which levers to pull to make change, a policymaker who can create systems and laws that protect and encourage, or a community member who can actively participate in solution development, you have the knowledge and power to make an impact. The tech that comes next can help ensure the impact is positive, one that strengthens communities without inflicting harm.

Chapter Nine
Where Will You Go Next?

In the course of writing this book we talked to so many talented, passionate, thoughtful people. In many of those conversations, we explained what we wanted to say in the book: the big ideas we wanted to get across; the reason for naming social impact organizations, technologists, funders, policymakers, and communities as the groups to think about; and the actions we hope people would take after reading it. We kept coming back to the same metaphor we envisioned at the beginning of working together:

> If all of us got together in one big room, and could pull out from our pockets the resources each of us has access to—be those skills, power, ideas, experience, or funding—we could pile it all up on the table. And, there, in front of us, would be everything we need to build anything we want: a new tool, a new program, a new world.

When we are together—truly, really, deeply together—we can do anything. The limits are our imagination and nothing else.

A COMMUNITY-CENTERED FUTURE IS POSSIBLE

Throughout the book we've highlighted the realities and outcomes surrounding us today, the products of systemic exclusion that impacts who is seen as worthy of or appropriate for leading change, developing technology, receiving funding, or creating policies. And, we've shared recommendations, asked questions, and highlighted examples of what it might look like to work differently, with an inverted system of inclusion instead.

The two illustrations in this book (introduced in chapters 1 and 2) clearly feel like opposites when we see them side by side, as they are shown on pages 198–199. It is our hope that, in some place in your life, you've felt the kind of openness and energy present in the second figure, *Future State: Systemic Inclusion*—that you have had even a brief experience of building something in intentional and inclusive spaces. Whatever the scope or the length of those opportunities, we can find confirmation in them that a community-centered future is possible.

Start by starting. There's no single place to begin. This book, like the work ahead of us, doesn't include a road map, a checklist, or a well-worn path. Instead, all of these ideas, recommendations, and examples are invitations for you to begin wherever you are with whatever resources you have—and to bring those resources near you along, too.

This book doesn't include trademarked business models or catchy new concepts because we want you to feel like reading this book is itself the practice of starting these conversations. There's no prerequisite, no certification, no membership needed to start reflecting on how each of us makes changes in how we do our work, and in how we deeply invest in our communities. There's no permission to be granted before each of us pushes these conversations into our organizations or our coalitions or our technology projects. There's no application process to be the one that commits to doing things in new ways.

If, in the process of exploring possibilities, you find yourself or your organization falling back to old limitations—placing application processes or requirements on who can engage, who can have ideas, or who can be part of the shift for what's next—pause to explore where those fallbacks derive from. Who and what is valued in those tired rubrics? And then remind yourself of who and what you want to value instead. Try to identify the barriers to collaboration, the beliefs that stop you from operating collectively. Commit yourself to transforming those values and easing those barriers into an environment that works for everyone, and begin again.

Allison Jones, a writer, speaker, and communications professional for social change, told us:[1]

> One of the things I learned during my time in tech is how big the tech space actually is. It touches and powers every part of our lives, which leaves it open to use and impact beyond the folks who work at tech companies. You have a wide range of people using tech. You have legislators monitoring tech, you have reporters covering tech, you have organizations pushing, supporting, collaborating, and arguing around various issues related to tech—from diversity, regulation, impact, and more. All of these examples represent various pressure points to get involved in shaping how tech can actually be used to make the world better. The key is to find where you can best fit in and commit yourself for the long haul.

The opportunity to build what is next is an opportunity for all of us. Inherent in the value of collective power and wisdom is the reminder that real change will be possible when building what is next includes all of us.

Technology is everywhere. Whether you are interested in arts or sports or early childhood development, in health or music or clean energy—technology has implications for what you do and how people

Current State: Systemic Exclusion

Future State: Systemic Inclusion

engage with it. Those implications include many factors related to equitable or inequitable access, participation, experience, and outcomes. Technology is an important entry point for addressing inequity across sectors and issues and communities. Shifting who makes technology, for what purpose, and where, can have dramatic results, as we have seen throughout this book.

This also means opportunity for change is everywhere. Certainly there will be lots of mistakes. Let's hope for mistakes that we can make early and identify clearly so that we can learn and improve as many times as possible. Let's commit to sharing those mistakes openly and learning collectively, so that every project can be better.

Let's get offline. After so much discussion of technology, digital tools, and the internet, it might be easy to think that the work ahead of us is online, through a screen, sent in packets across a network. Some of that work is—but so much of it isn't.

The work to change our world also needs time offline, in person, where we can build relationships, organize, and share, learn, and build together on a more human scale. Maybe we meet in an office or a park or a community center. Maybe we spend time together in each other's favorite café or restaurant. Maybe we introduce those we meet to those we think would enjoy collaborating. Maybe we laugh, and cry, and talk about our biggest dreams together.

WHAT WE NEED

The work ahead of us is massive. If it was easy it would exist already, right? We make no pretense that this will be fast, simple, or smooth. So, if we are preparing ourselves and each other for the hardest, longest, most complicated work we've ever done, it's important to be honest about what we need.

Space to imagine. If we ask you to close your eyes and imagine something—anything—you've never thought of before, it's not as easy as it sounds. That's because it's hard to imagine something so unlike what we've done before. Our minds are accustomed to referencing things we've already thought about. But we know the work ahead of us is to find new ways and create new models. This is going to stretch our imagination in new ways, too.

Many have a hard time picturing what a better world would look like or feel like—which can make the prospect of creating a better world seem impossible. We need to carve out time and space for ourselves to let our imagination expand, to allow ourselves to think about new options for our work today, but also new worlds for the future.

Space to try new things. We don't know which ideas will work and which won't. But before we try any of them, we need spaces where we can share ideas and talk about them together—long before we reach the stages of perfecting plans or scaling approaches.

Do you have an office or a meeting area that you can offer as a physical space where people can come together to test and try and collaborate? Are you a manager who can make sure staff have the space in their workloads and goals to be flexible, to pilot new options, and to operate in different ways?

What resources can you contribute to making the physical, emotional, personal, and professional space available to community members, collaborators, and potential partners? What power do you have to open up expectations, loosen timelines, or broaden requirements so that a diversity of options and a diversity of contributors can learn more together?

Space to rest. The more we practice something, the easier it becomes over time. But an important part of practicing anything is to regularly rest before resuming. But for some, meaningful space for rest—especially for communities navigating considerable historical and systemic oppressions, and for people working on essential missions—can be out of reach. And that rest is not just taking time off. Rest can be the reassurance of knowing the bills are paid, or that child care is available, or that adequate funding will cover all program expenses.

As we honor self-determination in program outcomes or service priorities, we need to also honor self-determination in what rest means and what rest requires. The question is not if we need and deserve rest, but how we can use collective resources to ensure that all of us have the space and time for regular rest.

Through all of this, remember that we are all connected. While you may ask for resources that someone else can support or enable, you can also be the one who has what someone else needs. As you reflect on where you want space made available for you and where you can provide it for others, think too about these same options at an organizational level—as well as in even broader ways, across geographies, across sectors, and across systems.

WHAT WE VALUE

In chapter 2, we outlined the values we prioritized in writing this book. We see these values as being essential to community-centered approaches to technology development and social impact. After we've identified and addressed the needs and options for changing the way technology is used, developed, and funded for social impact, as well as how we create policies and enable communities to be centered, it's important to come back to those same values:

1. An equitable world requires that we value the knowledge and wisdom of lived experience. The most affected individuals and communities need to be central to decisions about solutions and priorities.
2. An equitable world requires that we value the participation of a diversity of people in decision making, planning, and building technology—regardless of their technical knowledge or training.
3. An equitable world requires that we value accessibility as a priority from the start in all technology and social impact work.

4. An equitable world requires that we value the multiple ways that change is made, balancing the need to meet immediate challenges with a long view for how we can systemically eliminate those challenges.

5. An equitable world requires that we value the strength of collectively creating a vision of a better world. No single voice, visionary, or author of a future will work for everyone.

6. An equitable world requires that we value the dedication of individuals and communities in pursuing knowledge, experience, and skills. A diversity of people with deep training and practice offers valuable resources in collective efforts for change.

After reading this book, does anything feel different now? Do any of these values feel like less of a stretch to reach, and more of a core principle for your work? Do these values feel like your values? As we make progress toward our goal of an equitable world, these values may change and new values may emerge, but our need to orient to values that guide us will remain.

WE CAN BUILD TOGETHER

We aren't embellishing anything here—this is really what we believe: together, everything is possible.

The case studies and examples throughout this book varied widely in their technology tools and their communities, but all of them included people saying, "We can do this differently." All of them included people committing to prioritize the community and the benefit that could be created from doing so. From there, they found success, they found valuable outcomes, they found strength to do more.

Ours have not been exhaustive examples. Organizations and technology projects and community efforts that have produced similar results exist everywhere around the world. We hope you have your own examples—projects you've been part of, or even just know of. We hope that experience or reference powers you forward to be part of the examples we all learn from next.

The world we have today is filled with challenges. There are real hardships and injustices everywhere we look. It's because of this that we know that, together, we must commit to something else. Today, this moment, right now is the right time for us to take the next step toward a more equitable world, a world that works for all of us.

So, what will you build next?

Chapter Ten
Resources for What Comes Next

We all process information and ideas differently. We hope this book has pushed you to ask questions of yourself and those around you, and that it has inspired you to create opportunities for you to engage colleagues, partners, and potential collaborators in considering what you can change today as a first step to making even more change tomorrow. For many of us, discussion can be a rich platform for exploring our thoughts, developing our opinions, finding shared areas of interest, and discovering paths for moving thoughts into actions. To support a diversity of situations where this book may be read, used, and shared, we've collected here a set of discussion questions for teams, students, conferences, and collectives to use for reflection and dialogue, as well as a collation of the questions that appeared in each of the main chapters.

This is by no means meant to be an exhaustive list of the discussion points necessary for us to reimagine how we can work together. We simply hope these resources help you get started—and that you, your collaborators, and your community can progress from here.

QUESTIONS FOR DISCUSSION

Chapter 1: Where We Are and How We Got Here

- What concerns, hesitations, or biases about technology influence your relationship with digital tools?
- Where is technology a support or a barrier for you or your work today?
- How does the illustration of a private, polluted, siloed world compare to experiences you've had?

Chapter 2: Where Are We Going?

- How does the illustration of a sustainable, thriving, connected world compare to your work or experiences today?
- Do the values for an equitable world listed in chapter 2 feel similar to values your organization or communities have articulated already?
- Have you had experience with or know about technology services, applications, and/or tools that you feel harmed users? Can you imagine what it would be like to have technology services, applications, and tools that were accountable for the impact in your community?

Chapter 3: Changing Technology Inside Social Impact Organizations

- How can organizations gain clarity about their mission so that they may identify ways technology can extend it?
- What concrete actions can social impact organizations take to create a culture that embraces technology?
- What have you learned through your own technology projects, attempts, or investments that you can share with others?

Chapter 4: Changing Technology Development

- When might organizations want to develop new technology instead of buying existing technology?
- How does discrimination appear in data and technology systems?
- What are some ways technologists could expand their technical expertise and their translation skills?

Chapter 5: Changing Technology and Social Impact Funding

- How should funders think about the return on their investment?
- What are ways to maximize a "double bottom line" for funders?
- How would you structure a funding arrangement to allow for community involvement and maintenance support?

Chapter 6: Changing Laws and Policies

- Which side of the "policy about technology" versus the "technology for policy" spectrum most resonates with you?
- Is it problematic to have coders as de facto policymakers? Or could that be a way to broaden the pool of policymakers? How might coders be held accountable for their policy decisions?
- Identify a social challenge that is important to you. In order to try to create an opening for change, what policymaking body might you want to build a relationship with? What other organizations might you want to build a coalition with?

Chapter 7: Changing Access to Social Impact Technology

- What could it look like to pool funding, technical skills and knowledge, and other resources within a community?
- What social infrastructure are you part of, and how could you bring others in?

- Interoperability is the concept that new products or services should be able to be used with and alongside existing products. In what ways could interoperability make it easier for communities and social impact organizations to adopt technology?

Chapter 8: Start Building Power for What's Next

- Consider the groups that you are part of. What else is needed for what comes next?
- What resistance to change can you anticipate getting from your colleagues, partners, or potential collaborators? How might you address that resistance?
- In the process of building power for change, who can you identify as allies to help you?

Chapter 9: Where Will You Go Next?

- The process of change requires support. What do you most need in order to make a change in yourself? In your organization? What about in broader communities or systems you're connected to?
- What resources can you offer to others to provide space or support for their needs?
- What are you ready to do tomorrow?

QUESTIONS TO ASK OTHERS

In chapters 3 through 7, we included questions to start conversations with others about where values may be aligned for community-centered work, where barriers may exist to prevent that work, and where new approaches may emerge. To follow are those same questions, reorganized by group.

Questions for What Comes Next: Social Impact Organizations

If you work in a social impact organization, here are questions to help you push your work and our world forward.

Ask your peers:

- What tech tools are working well for you to manage projects? For managing constituents? What tools didn't live up to the hype?
- Do you use a change-management process when rolling out a new technology internally?
- What needs are you still trying to address for your staff?
- How do you ensure your staff knows how to use and continually uses technology?
- Where do you seek information on what tech is useful for social impact organizations and how to adopt that tech into your organization?

Ask technologists:

- How have you learned about our particular work and affected communities? How will our communities be included in the design and testing processes?
- What happens if your technology fails? Who will be harmed?
- How will you ensure that I understand how the systems are being used? How the data is being used?
- How will you ensure that your technology will work with what technology and systems we have today? How will you ensure that the cost to maintain your technology won't be prohibitive for us?
- How will you ensure that your work advances at a reasonable pace, that it respects the organization's time, and that it's ultimately delivered on time?

Ask funders:

- It's important to us that we retain both oversight and control of our work. And while we will report what outcomes your funding would enable us to produce, that reporting will not be granular. Are you ready to provide funding while also respecting our methods?
- Can you support adequate funding to bring more development staff and teams into social impact organizations?
- What experience or history do you have with the communities we work with?
- How will you support us in honoring the self-determination of our program participants and community members?
- How do you respond to failure? Are you open to shared learning?

Ask policymakers:

- It's important to us that you fully understand the issues we know about and the priorities of the communities who are part of our work. How do we best educate you on those points?
- How do you help us navigate policymaking systems to ensure our efforts are successful? How will you help us know to engage and when?
- What have been successful strategies for organizations and communities advocating for new policies?
- Can you describe who and what influences your policies?
- How can we better work together on proactive policies that enable as many people and organizations as possible to be part of change-making work?

Ask the communities you work with:

- Do you have positive or negative examples of working with a social impact organization? If so, what are they?

- Who in your community are the key decision makers who must be brought along with any change?
- Are there decision-making or planning norms and expectations that we can honor and follow?
- What privileges, power, or access can be extended in service to your priorities?
- What are your biggest priorities within our mission?

Questions for What Comes Next: Technologists

If you are a technologist or work for a technology development company, here are questions to help you push your work and our world forward.

Ask those in social impact organizations:

- What does "technology" mean to your organization? Who on your staff is comfortable discussing how to use tech to improve their operations?
- Do you have documented processes for how you work with staff and with clients? If not, are you open to creating this documentation?
- Who are the champions for technology in the organization? Who are the champions in each team?
- How are community members involved in decision making within the organization? How can we increase community-member input into technology projects?
- How is technology addressed in your strategic plan? How do these plans meet that strategic goal?

Ask of your peers:

- Did you partner with organizations and individuals throughout design, development, and testing?

- How did you determine that this solution you propose is the right approach? What did you decide not to do and why?
- What lessons do you have to share on building capacity and leadership in the community that will be maintaining the technology?
- What specific tools and techniques were applicable in this situation and why? Do you have code to share?
- Are there solutions that you developed here that could be used elsewhere? What organizations or individuals can we consult to make that happen?

Ask funders:

- Are you willing to provide enough funding for us to (a) hire team members from affected communities and (b) support their technical and professional development in this project?
- Are you ready to fund us with a long-term commitment so we can ensure we provide support, maintenance, and ongoing improvements after launch?
- How will you support us in retaining access to our intellectual property so we can continue to learn and use it elsewhere?
- What is your comfort level with slower return on investment so that we can be purposeful in engagement and development?
- Are you committed to funding for inclusive processes that include slower development timelines and compensation to participants?

Ask policymakers:

- How can we proactively understand current and forthcoming policy decisions? How can we help inform definitions within upcoming policies intentionally to ensure community adoption and protection?
- How can we build technologies in support of collaborative and participatory policymaking?
- How can we best share what we've learned and describe the barriers we face so as to inform and influence policymaking?

- How can you best inform us about community priorities and needs from other issues areas?
- How can we work together to adopt privacy and security priorities for all of our policies?

Ask the communities who benefit from or are affected by your technologies:

- What level of tech literacy/proficiency does your community have? What would you like it to be?
- What support or resources would you need to have to view participating in the development process as useful?
- In what ways has this community been harmed or negatively affected by technology?
- Who would be harmed if the technology we build fails?
- Who will profit and benefit the most from the technology we build?

Questions for What Comes Next: Funders

If you are part of a funding organization or are an individual investor, here are questions to help you push your work and our world forward.

Ask those in social impact organizations:

- What is the next internal process you want to either (a) develop and apply technology to, or (b) improve the technology for?
- What percentage of your staff participates in either gathering requirements or defining user stories? What percentage of your staff participates in testing?
- Do you have the internal capacity to deploy tech? Or do you need to be connected to (provided with?) a service that deploys tech for social impact organizations?
- In what ways are you engaging community members so as to ensure these technologies relevantly address their priorities?
- What have you learned from previous iterations or attempts similar to this one that can be brought into this next attempt?

Ask technologists:

- What are the expected long-term maintenance needs for the technology?
- How will you teach the organization staff how to interact with and maintain what you develop?
- What support will the organization need to make successful maintenance happen?
- Based on what you learn in the design process, how will you communicate if changes are needed?
- How are you connected to the communities impacted by this project? How will they be involved?

Ask of your peers:

- If you spent down the fund, how much faster could you meet your mission and accelerate impact in your funding region?
- What steps do you take to staff your organization inclusively?
- How are you investing in your staff's tech knowledge and capacity?
- How can we work together to create a pool of funding that is turned over for community ownership?
- How are you leveraging all of your organization's assets—beyond grants—in order to meet the mission?

Ask policymakers:

- How can our resources be combined with yours to accelerate or ensure participatory processes?
- What public–private partnerships could be established in service to the internet and technology development needs in our communities?
- How can we share what we've learned and tried with new models and efforts so as to support emerging policies?

- How can we surface and share successful stories from other regions or sectors in order to inform new policies?
- Are there potential gaps in available knowledge or data that we could resource for research and evaluation?

Ask of the communities affected or involved:

- We believe that we could enable funding outside of established organizational structures if we established trust. How can we do that?
- How can we collaborate on new models of ownership for technologies developed in the community with our funding?
- How will you tell the story of this work or project to share what you learn with others?
- How have you already tried or tested this project? What other projects are ready for investment?
- What expectations should we set for return on investment?

Questions for What Comes Next: Policymakers

If you are a policymaker, here are questions to help you push your work and our world forward.

Ask those in social impact organizations:

- How are you working in coalition to surface priorities?
- What examples or proof of concept do you have from your community/work that makes clear working in coalition is a priority?
- What data do you have that supports harm reduction in policies for your community?
- Can you help us understand why this hasn't gone through/been successful in the past?
- What other policies do you feel are successful that we could scale or learn from?

Ask technologists:

- How have you ensured people will be able to access your technical solution?
- How have you mitigated bias in your technical solution's development and implementation?
- Where does the tech solution end and the need for new policies begin? In other words, what are the limits of the technical solution?
- Where are the components of the technology that are not currently protected or directed by policy?
- How does this technology maintain protections for the user's ability to control their data?

Ask funders:

- What policies or other legal mechanisms would most catalyze your institution to increase the amount of funding distributed?
- Can you commit to being part of policy accountability?
- What can we do to encourage your participation in public–private–community partnerships?
- How can we work together to extend initiatives toward accessibility and equity in your community?
- How are you working in cross-sector collaborations to surface priorities?

Ask your peers:

- How do you verify and validate your information sources?
- How are you actively working to remove bias in your policymaking process?
- What participatory processes have been successful for you?
- How can we best share community priorities and needs from different policy topic areas?
- How are you reporting back on progress and challenges in policymaking initiatives?

Ask communities affected or benefited:

- What technologies or services do you not currently have access to, either because of availability or affordability?
- What experiences or knowledge do you have that you could share with us for better policymaking?
- It's important to us that we stay in communication with you and your community in a manner that honors individuals' needs and time commitments and is accessible to all. How can we best do that?
- How can we best elevate your voices and stories in the policymaking process without being extractive?
- What can we do to support community access and participation in policymaking?

Questions for What Comes Next: Communities

If you are a community member outside of the above organizations, here are questions to help you push your goals and our world forward.

Ask those in social impact organizations:

- How will your systems, data policies, and practices honor our expectations for consent, opt-ins, and safe and secure data?
- How do you support us advocating for ourselves? How can we continue to own our stories and experience with you?
- How is our lived experience centered in decision making?
- What structures are available to formalize our leadership in the organization?
- How do we contribute to setting the organization's goals?

Ask technologists:

- How can our lived experience be prioritized in the design and development of the tech?
- How will you invest in our training and knowledge so that we can be part of ownership in the long term?

- How will you ensure I understand how the systems and data are being used? How will you ensure I control the way my data is being used?
- How will you ensure our consent will be requested (now and in the future) in relation to the ways data is used to make decisions for and about us?
- What's the plan for making sure we can continue to use this technology after you're not involved?

Ask funders:

- How do we build trust with you so that our solutions can be prioritized?
- It's important to us to influence who gets approval to work in our community. How can we partner with you on that?
- It's important to us that your strategic planning and portfolio priorities reflect the lived realities and needs of our community. How can we best share our priorities with you? How does our feedback factor into your definition and expectation of return on investment?
- Are you committed to funding solutions working with groups that are not designated 501(c)(3) or another equivalent registered charity organization?
- It is important to us that we are engaged as early as possible. How will community engagement take place prior to decisions about what or who to fund?

Ask policymakers:

- How can we work together to change policies so as to increase funders' annual distributions?
- How might policy support new mechanisms for providing resources to our community?
- How can we work together to build policy protections for communities, individuals, and users?

- How can policies better force accountability among users and technology providers and social impact service providers?
- If any technology harms come from there being a lack of policy, are you prepared to be accountable for that?

Ask each other:

- How did you get started?
- What have you tried? What have you learned? What's worth repeating or reusing?
- In pushing for change, technology development, or other investment, how did you decide what work to take on and what not to take on?
- What are our dreams?
- What resources do we already have that we can use?

RECOMMENDED READING & ADDITIONAL RESOURCES

We hope this book was a valuable tool in your personal work to build what comes next. To add to that we created a website to share the many additional books, reports, research projects, and other resources that we consider relevant to the collective work of changing the world. For those including the book in your courses and training programs, we also developed training aids and discussion templates for making this book actionable for you and your community. You can find those there as well. For more, please visit https://TheTechThatComesNext.com.

Notes

CHAPTER 1

1. Daniel Victor, "Microsoft Created a Twitter Bot to Learn from Users. It Quickly Became a Racist Jerk," *New York Times* (March 24, 2016), https://www.nytimes.com/2016/03/25/technology/microsoft-created-a-twitter-bot-to-learn-from-users-it-quickly-became-a-racist-jerk.html.

2. Jenn Stroud Rossmann, "Public Thinker: Virginia Eubanks on Digital Surveillance and Power," *Public Books* (July 9, 2020), https://www.publicbooks.org/public-thinker-virginia-eubanks-on-digital-surveillance-and-people-power/.

3. Melvin Kranzberg, "Technology and History: 'Kranzberg's Laws," *Technology and Culture 27*, no. 3 (July 1986): 544–60, https://www.jstor.org/stable/3105385.

4. Sanjana Varghese, "Ruha Benjamin: We Definitely Can't Wait for Silicon Valley to Become More Diverse," *The Guardian* (June 29, 2019), https://www.theguardian.com/technology/2019/jun/29/ruha-benjamin-we-cant-wait-silicon-valley-become-more-diverse-prejudice-algorithms-data-new-jim-code.

5. Erik Gregersen, "History of Technology Timeline," *Encyclopedia Britannica*, accessed September 1, 2021, https://www.britannica.com/story/history-of-technology-timeline.

6. Meredith Broussard, *Artificial Unintelligence: How Computers Misunderstand the World* (Cambridge: MA: MIT Press, 2019), 8.

CHAPTER 2

1. Gabriel Kasper et al., "COVID-19 Scenario Planning for Nonprofit and Philanthropic Organizations," Deloitte, July 2020, https://www2.deloitte.com/us/en/pages/about-deloitte/articles/covid-19-planning-scenarios-for-social-sector-organizations.html.

CHAPTER 3

1. NTEN, "2020 Tech Accelerate Report" (November 25, 2020), https://www.nten.org/article/2020-tech-accelerate-report/.
2. Salesforce, "2nd Edition Nonprofit Trends Report," accessed October 11, 2021, https://www.salesforce.org/nonprofit/download-2nd-edition-nonprofit-trends-report/.
3. Salesforce, "2nd Edition Nonprofit Trends Report," accessed October 11, 2021, https://www.salesforce.org/nonprofit/download-2nd-edition-nonprofit-trends-report/.
4. NTEN, "2020 Data Empowerment Report" (November 25, 2020), https://www.nten.org/article/2020-data-empowerment-report/.
5. Edima Elinegwinga, Zoom interview with Amy Sample Ward (September 22, 2021). Visit the ZERO TO THREE website at https://www.zerotothree.org/.
6. Pew Research Center, "Americans with disabilities less likely than those without to own some digital devices," September 10, 2021, https://www.pewresearch.org/fact-tank/2021/09/10/americans-with-disabilities-less-likely-than-those-without-to-own-some-digital-devices/.
7. Web Accessibility Initiative, "Web Content Accessibility Guidelines (WCAG) Overview," accessed September 1, 2021, https://www.w3.org/WAI/standards-guidelines/wcag/.
8. WebAIM, "We Have Web Accessibility in Mind," accessed September 1, 2021, https://webaim.org/.
9. Funraise and Nonprofit Tech For Good, "Global NGO Technology Report 2019" (2019), https://funraise.org/techreport/.
10. NTEN, "Technology-Enabled Operations Report" (February 2021), https://www.nten.org/article/2021-technology-enabled-operations-report/
11. Mala Kumar, Zoom interview with Amy Sample Ward (September 23, 2021). Visit the GitHub Social Impact website at https://socialimpact.github.com/.

CHAPTER 4

1. Zip Recruiter, "What Is the Difference Between a Technologist and a Technician," accessed September 1, 2021, https://www.ziprecruiter.com/e/What-Is-the-Difference-Between-a-Technologist-and-a-Technician.

2. DataKind, "Improving College Success Through Predictive Modeling," April 2017, https://www.datakind.org/projects/improving-college-success-through-predictive-modeling.

3. Michael Dowd, interview with Afua Bruce (October 11, 2021).

4. Taken from CUSP Overview Document, collaboratively written by several staff and faculty at John Jay College, and shared in email with Afua Bruce (October 4, 2021).

5. Rob Price, "Apple and Google Partnered to Develop Contact-tracing Apps to Fight COVID-19—But They Fizzled in the US Because People Barely Used Them," Business Insider (August 26, 2021), https://www.businessinsider.com/apple-google-contact-tracing-apps-barely-used-in-us-investigation-2021-8.

6. Tulane University School of Public Health and Tropical Medicine blog, "Understanding the Effects of Social Isolation on Mental Health." Dec 8, 2020 https://publichealth.tulane.edu/blog/effects-of-social-isolation-on-mental-health/.

7. Michael Dowd, interview with Afua Bruce, October 11, 2021.

8. Isobel Asher Hamilton, "Amazon Built an AI Tool to Hire People But Had to Shut It Down Because It Was Discriminating Against Women," Business Insider (October 10, 2018), https://www.businessinsider.com/amazon-built-ai-to-hire-people-discriminated-against-women-2018-10.

9. Ernest Hamilton, "AccessiBe's Search Engine accessFind Is Launched to Help Those with Disabilities Find Accessible Websites," Tech Times (June 14, 2021), https://www.techtimes.com/articles/261437/20210614/accessibes-search-engine-accessfind-is-launched-to-help-those-with-disabilities-find-accessible-websites.htm.

10. U.S. Equal Employment Opportunity Commission, "Diversity in High Tech," accessed September 1, 2021, https://www.eeoc.gov/special-report/diversity-high-tech.

11. Kate Rooney and Yasmin Khorram, "Tech Companies Say They Value Diversity, But Reports Show Little Change in Last Six Years," CNBC (June 12, 2020), https://www.cnbc.com/2020/06/12/six-years-into-diversity-reports-big-tech-has-made-little-progress.html.

12. Daisy Magnus-Aryitey, Zoom interview with Afua Bruce (September 7, 2021). Visit the Code the Dream Website at https://codethedream.org/about/.

13. RedHat, "What Is Open Source" (October 14, 2019), https://www.redhat.com/en/topics/open-source/what-is-open-source.

14. "Exploring Community Technology: Who Owns Our Technology," Community Technology Field Guide, accessed September 1, 2021, https://community technology.github.io/docs/intro-ct/investigate-tech/.

15. Lisa Nakamura, "The Internet Is a Trash Fire. Here's How to Fix It," accessed September 1, 2021, https://www.ted.com/talks/lisa_nakamura_the_internet_is_a_trash_fire_here_s_how_to_fix_it.

16. Kathy Pham, email to Afua Bruce (October 5, 2021).

17. "Welcome to Public Interest Cybersecurity" (https://www.citizenclinic.io, last updated November 17, 2020) and "Case Studies" (last updated July 26, 2020, https://www.citizenclinic.io/Case_Studies/), The Citizen Clinic Cybersecurity Education Center, Center for Long-Term Cybersecurity, University of California, Berkeley.

18. Tayo Fabusuyi, Jessica Taketa, and Raymar Hampshire, "Building Career Pathways for Diverse Public Interest Technology Entrepreneurs," New America, last updated June 30, 2021, https://www.newamerica.org/pit/reports/building-career-pathways-for-diverse-public-interest-technology-entrepreneurs/findings/.

CHAPTER 5

1. Chantal Forster, email interview with Amy Sample Ward (September 22, 2021).

2. "Building a Movement of Corporate Philanthropy," Pledge 1%, accessed October 11, 2021, https://pledge1percent.org/.

3. Center for Civil Society Studies, "The 2019 Nonprofit Employment Report (2019)" (January 17, 2019), http://ccss.jhu.edu/publications-findings/?did=507.

4. International Day of NGOs. "What Is an NGO?," accessed September 1, 2021, https://worldngoday.org/what-is-an-ngo/.

5. Aki Shibuya, email interview with Amy Sample Ward (September 19, 2021).

6. Candid, "What Is a Program-related Investment?," accessed September 1, 2021, https://learning.candid.org/resources/knowledge-base/pris/.

7. Nonprofit Quarterly, "Trouble in Paradigm: Foundations' Bargain with the Devil," June 30, 2021, https://nonprofitquarterly.org/trouble-in-paradigm-foundations-bargain-with-the-devil/.

8. Original footnote as published in *Nonprofit Quarterly*: "A relatively small group of US private foundations have gone 'all in' for mission, aligning their portfolios with their social aims, despite Heron's early demonstration of its feasibility.

By December 2016, Heron had shifted 100 percent of assets to mission. See Charles Ewald, Heidi Patel, and Jaclyn Foroughi, The F.B. Heron Foundation: 100 Percent for Mission—and Beyond, Stanford, CA: Stanford Business, 2018, accessed June 19, 2021."

9. Original footnote as published in *Nonprofit Quarterly*: "The financial data contained herein both of salaries and foundation assets is based on author's compilation of information from GuideStar published tax filings based on foundation fiscal-year 2018 data."

10. MacArthur Foundation, "Aligning Our Investments With Our Mission, Values, and Programs," September 22, 2021, https://www.macfound.org/press/perspectives/aligning-our-investments-with-our-mission-values-and-programs.

11. Feeding America, "Facts About Hunger in America," accessed September 1, 2021, https://www.feedingamerica.org/hunger-in-america.

12. National Center for Charitable Statistics, "The Nonprofit Sector in Brief" (June 18, 2020), https://nccs.urban.org/project/nonprofit-sector-brief.

13. Independent Sector, "The Charitable Sector," accessed September 1, 2021, https://independentsector.org/about/the-charitable-sector/.

14. CB Insights, "386 Startup Failure Post-Mortems" (September 28, 2021), https://www.cbinsights.com/research/startup-failure-post-mortem/.

15. Mala Kumar, Zoom interview with Amy Sample Ward (September 23, 2021).

16. Jenny Kassan, email interview with Amy Sample Ward (August 6, 2021).

17. Wilneida Negrón, email interview with Afua Bruce (September 30, 2021).

18. Parity, "Welcome to Parity," accessed September 1, 2021, https://www.parity-fund.com/.

19. Women Who Tech, "We Break Down Barriers and Get More Women Startups Funded," accessed September 1, 2021, https://womenwhotech.org/about.

20. May First Movement Technology, "Why You Should Join," accessed September 1, 2021, https://mayfirst.coop/en/why-join/.

CHAPTER 6

1. Afua Bruce and Maria Filippelli, "Tech Companies Need a History Lesson and Civil Rights Groups Can Provide It," *The Hill* (March 29, 2019), https://thehill.com/opinion/technology/436464-tech-companies-need-a-history-lesson-and-civil-rights-organizations-can.

2. "About NDIA," National Digital Inclusion Alliance, accessed September 1, 2021, https://www.digitalinclusion.org/about-ndia/.

3. United States Senator Murray Working for Washington State, "Senators Murray, Portman, and King Introduce Major Bipartisan Legislation to Close Digital Divide, Promote Digital Equity," Press release (June 10, 2019), https://www.murray.senate.gov/public/index.cfm/newsreleases?ID=0EBFF33F-29C4-44CB-A4BD-6B1B1C986794.

4. Angela Seifer, Zoom interview with Amy Sample Ward (September 28, 2021).

5. Angela Seifer, Zoom interview with Amy Sample Ward (September 28, 2021). Visit NDIA's website at https://www.digitalinclusion.org/.

6. "The Digital Equity Act," #DigitalEquityNow, accessed October 8, 2021, https://www.digitalequityact.org/.

7. "About Us," Rural Community Assistance Partnership, accessed September 1, 2021, https://www.rcap.org/about/.

8. "What Is the Farm Bill," National Sustainable Agricultural Coalition, accessed September 1, 2021, https://sustainableagriculture.net/our-work/campaigns/fbcampaign/what-is-the-farm-bill/.

9. Cecilia Munoz and Nathan Ohle, "Want Better Policy? Bring in the Technologists," *The Hill* (January 29, 2019), https://thehill.com/opinion/technology/427504-want-better-policy-bring-in-the-technologists?rl=1.

10. Nathan Ohle, Zoom interview with Afua Bruce (September 24, 2021). Visit RCAP's website at https://www.rcap.org/.

11. Rural Innovation Stronger Economy (RISE) Grants, USDA Rural Development, accessed October 11, 2021, https://www.rd.usda.gov/programs-services/business-programs/rural-innovation-stronger-economy-rise-grants.

12. Maurice Turner, Zoom interview with Afua Bruce (September 24, 2021).

13. Nicol Turner Lee, "Closing the Digital and Economic Divides in Rural America," accessed September 1, 2021, https://www.brookings.edu/longform/closing-the-digital-and-economic-divides-in-rural-america/.

14. Bill Callahan, "AT&T's Digital Redlining of Cleveland," Blog entry (March 10, 2017), https://www.digitalinclusion.org/blog/2017/03/10/atts-digital-redlining-of-cleveland/.

15. "Internet Access Advocates Say AT&T Is Guilty of 'Digital Redlining' in Some Cleveland Neighborhoods," *News5 Cleveland* (March 12, 2017), https://www.news5cleveland.com/news/local-news/oh-cuyahoga/atts-digital-redlining-of-cleveland-neighborhoods.

16. "Rep Clarke Introduces the Anti-Digital Redlining Act of 2021 with Baltimorean Support," *Benton Institute for Broadband and Society* (August 10, 2021), https://www.benton.org/headlines/rep-clarke-introduces-anti-digital-redlining-act-2021-baltimorean-support.

17. "Emergency Broadband Benefit," Federal Communications Commission, accessed September 1, 2021, https://www.fcc.gov/broadbandbenefit.

18. "FTC Bans SpyFone and CEO from Surveillance Business and Orders Company to Delete All Secretly Stolen Data," Federal Trade Commission, press release (September 1, 2021), https://www.ftc.gov/news-events/press-releases/2021/09/ftc-bans-spyfone-and-ceo-from-surveillance-business.

19. "5 Examples of Public Private Partnerships in Implementation," NMBL Strategies (September 12, 2019), https://www.nmblstrategies.com/blog/5-examples-of-public-private-partnerships-in-implementation.

20. Maurice Turner, Zoom interview with Afua Bruce (September 24, 2021).

21. Brad Smith and Carol Ann Browne, "Tech Firms Need More Regulation," *The Atlantic* (September 9, 2019), https://www.theatlantic.com/ideas/archive/2019/09/please-regulate-us/597613/.

22. Jamie Condliffe, "Big Tech Says It Wants Government to Regulate AI. Here's Why," February 12, 2020, https://www.protocol.com/ai-amazon-microsoft-ibm-regulation.

23. Sintia Radu, "The World Wants More Tech Regulation," *US News & World Report* (January 15, 2020), https://www.usnews.com/news/best-countries/articles/2020-01-15/the-world-wants-big-tech-companies-to-be-regulated.

24. Larry Downes, "How More Regulation for U.S. Tech Could Backfire," *Harvard Business Review* (February 9, 2018), https://hbr.org/2018/02/how-more-regulation-for-u-s-tech-could-backfire.

25. "What We Do," Federal Communications Commission, accessed September 1, 2021, https://www.fcc.gov/about-fcc/what-we-do.

26. "About the FTC," Federal Trade Commission, accessed September 1, 2021, https://www.ftc.gov/about-ftc.

27. "Google Searches Expose Racial Bias, Says Study of Names," *BBC News Service* (February 4, 2013), https://www.bbc.com/news/technology-21322183.

28. "Our Work," Upturn: Toward Justice and Technology, accessed September 1, 2021, https://www.upturn.org/work/.

29. Cecilia Munoz and Nathan Ohle, "Want Better Policy? Bring in the Technologists" *The Hill* (January 29, 2019), https://thehill.com/opinion/technology/427504-want-better-policy-bring-in-the-technologists?rl=1.

30. "About MDS," Open Mobility Foundation, accessed September 1, 2021, https://www.openmobilityfoundation.org/about-mds/.

31. "Civic User Testing Group," CityTech Collaborative, accessed September 1, 2021, https://www.citytech.org/cutgroup.

32. Anjali Tripathi, email to Afua Bruce (October 10, 2021).

33. Justin King and Afua Bruce, "Voices from the Social Safety Net," *Slate* (February 28, 2019), https://slate.com/technology/2019/02/snap-freshebt-benefits-technology-voice.html.

34. "Travis Moore's Written Testimony Before Congress," TechCongress (April 28, 2021), https://www.techcongress.io/blog/2021/4/28/travis-moores-written-testimony-before-the-select-committee-on-the-modernization-of-congress-united-states-house-of-representativesnbsp.

35. "About Us," TechCongress, accessed September 1, 2021, https://www.techcongress.io/about-us.

36. "Medicare Data API: Blue Button and Data at the Point of Care," U.S. Digital Service (September 1, 2021), https://www.usds.gov/projects/blue-button-2.

37. "Discharge Status Upgrade Tool," U.S. Digital Service, accessed September 1, 2021, https://www.usds.gov/projects/discharge-upgrade-tool.

38. Laura Manley, email to Afua Bruce and Amy Sample Ward (September 10, 2021).

39. Apritha Peteru and Sabrina Hersi Issa, "Toward Ethical Technology: Framing Human Rights in the Future of Digital Innovation," *RightsXTech* (October 2021).

40. Apritha Peteru and Sabrina Hersi Issa, "Toward Ethical Technology."

41. Brandon Forester, interview with Afua Bruce (September 24, 2021).

CHAPTER 7

1. Chris Worman, email interview with Amy Sample Ward (September 21, 2021). Visit the Connect Humanity website at https://connecthumanity.fund/.

2. Vanice Dunn, email interview with Amy Sample Ward (September 28, 2021).

3. Dr. Fallon Wilson, email interview with Afua Bruce (September 27, 2021).

4. BroadbandNow, "BroadbandNow Estimates Availability for all 50 States; Confirms that More than 42 Million Americans Do Not Have Access to Broadband" (August 29, 2021), https://broadbandnow.com/research/fcc-broadband-overreporting-by-state.

5. Motherboard, "New Data Says More Communities Built Their Own Broadband Because of COVID" (September 10, 2021), https://www.vice.com/en/article/7kv3ge/new-data-says-more-communities-built-their-own-broadband-because-of-covid.

6. "About MuralNet," MuralNet, accessed September 1, 2021, https://www .muralnet.org/about/.

7. "MuralNet and Cisco Launch Sustainable Tribal Networks Program," MuralNet (September 9, 2020), https://www.muralnet.org/2020/09/muralnet-and-cisco-launch-sustainable/.

8. Lyel Rener, email interview with Afua Bruce (September 27, 2021).

9. Sabrina Roach, Zoom interview with Amy Sample Ward (September 27, 2021).

10. Sam Chenkin, email interview with Amy Sample Ward (September 27, 2021).

CHAPTER 8

1. Brandon Forrester, Conversation with Afua Bruce (September 24, 2021).

2. Urban Affairs Association. "Michelle M. Thompson (University of New Orleans) Coordinates WhoData.org" (August 1, 2013), https://urbanaffairsassociation .org/2013/08/01/michelle-m-thompson-university-of-new-orleans-coordinates-whodata-org/.

3. Michelle Thompson, email to Afua Bruce (September 25, 2021).

4. "Our Purpose," BlackTechFutures Research Institute, accessed September 1, 2021, https://www.blacktechfutures.com/.

5. Dr. Fallon Wilson, email to Afua Bruce and Amy Sample Ward (September 27, 2021).

6. Quincy Brown, email to Afua Bruce and Amy Sample Ward (August 27, 2021).

7. Lyel Resner, interview with Afua Bruce (September 27, 2021).

CHAPTER 9

1. Allison Jones, email interview with Amy Sample Ward (September 30, 2021).

Index